MUSICAL INSTRUMENTS

COMPILED BY TONY CURTIS

While every care has been taken in compiling the information contained in this volume the publishers cannot accept any liability for loss, financial or otherwise, incurred by reliance placed on the information herein.

First Published March 1977
Reprinted   Nov   1977
Revised Edition June 1978

Exchange rate $2 = £1 or rate
of exchange at time of auction.

Original Edition   ISBN 902921-50-9
Revised Edition   ISBN 902921-78-9

Copyright © Lyle Publications 1977.
Published by Lyle Publications, Glenmayne, Galashiels, Scotland.
Distributed in the U.S.A. by Apollo, 391 South Road, Poughkeepsie, N.Y. 12601.

INTRODUCTION

Congratulations! You now have in your hands an extremely valuable book. It is one of a series specially devised to aid the busy professional dealer in his everyday trading. It will also prove to be of great value to all collectors and those with goods to sell, for it is crammed with illustrations, brief descriptions and valuations of hundreds of antiques.

Every effort has been made to ensure that each specialised volume contains the widest possible variety of goods in its particular category though the greatest emphasis is placed on the middle bracket of trade goods rather than on those once - in - a - lifetime museum pieces whose values are of academic rather than practical interest to the vast majority of dealers and collectors.

This policy has been followed as a direct consequence of requests from dealers who sensibly realise that, no matter how comprehensive their knowledge, there is always a need for reliable, up-to-date reference works for identification and valuation purposes.

When using your Antiques and their Values to assess the worth of goods, please bear in mind that it would be impossible to place upon any item a precise value which would hold good under all circumstances. No antique has an exactly calculable value; its price is always the result of a compromise reached between buyer and seller, and questions of condition, local demand and the business acumen of the parties involved in a sale are all factors which affect the assessment of an object's 'worth' in terms of hard cash.

In the final analysis, however, such factors cancel out when large numbers of sales are taken into account by an experienced valuer, and it is possible to arrive at a surprisingly accurate assessment of current values of antiques; an assessment which may be taken confidently to be a fair indication of the worth of an object and which provides a reliable basis for negotiation.

Throughout this book, objects are grouped under category headings and, to expedite reference, they progress in price order within their own categories. Where the description states 'one of a pair' the value given is that for the pair sold as such.

Printed by Apollo Press, Dominion Way, Worthing, Sussex, England.
Bound by Newdigate Press, Vincent Lane, Dorking, Surrey, England.

CONTENTS

Automaton Figures 8	Music Stands 49
Accordions. 10	Miscellaneous 50
American Fiddle 10	Musical Boxes. 52
Bagpipes 10	Oboes 61
Banjos. 11	Ocarina 61
Barrel Organs 12	Octavino 62
Bows. .14	Operaphone 62
Bugles 19	Ophicleides 62
Cecilium 20	Orphica 62
Ceterone 20	Organs. 63
Cellos .20	Phonographs. 65
Chitarrone 21	Pianos 71
Cor Anglais 21	Pianino 85
Cornets 21	Piccolo 85
Clarinets 22	Pochette 85
Clavichords 23	Polyphones 86
Cornopean 24	Radios. 88
Couenophone. 24	Recorders 88
Drums. 25	Regal 89
Esrar. .27	Sackbut. 89
Euphonium 27	Salterio Tedesco 89
Fagottino. 27	Sarrusophone 89
Flageolet 27	Serpents 90
Flutes .28	Sitar .90
Gramophones 30	Spinets 91
Guitars 36	Symphonion Accordion 92
Harmonicor 38	Symphonion. 92
Harmonium 39	Tibetan Horns. 93
Harps .39	Trumpets. 94
Harpsichords 42	Viols. 95
Horns .44	Violas 95
Hurdy Gurdies 46	Violins, Mute 99
Kits 46	Violins 99
Lutes .46	Violin Cases 118
Lyres .47	Violoncellos 119
Mandoras 47	Virginals 122
Mandolins 48	Zithers 122

AUTOMATON FIGURES

Early 20th century French musical automaton group of three clowns, 1ft.4in. high. $300 £150

An amusing English cat tea party automaton, the cardboard construction operated by a clockwork mechanism at the rear. $310 £155

17in. doll, whose head moves as her hands play the piano, which is really a musical box. $1,150 £575

Musical automaton by E. Jumeau, 21in. high. $1,600 £800

A good late 19th century French musician automaton, 1ft.10in. wide. $1,680 £840

Late 19th century French musical ballerina automaton, 1ft.10in. high. $1,800 £900

AUTOMATON FIGURES

A good French musician automaton, the figure with composition head, wearing a scarlet long tailed coat, circa 1900, 1ft.11in. high. $1,800 £900

Early 20th century French dancing girl automaton, the bisque headed doll with glass eyes, 1ft.10in. high. $1,920 £960

A French musical pianist automaton with plaque G. Vichy Fils, 1ft.3in. wide, circa 1900. $2,050 £1,025

Late 19th century French cymbalist automaton, the bisque headed doll impressed on the back VTE Jumeau S.O.D.G. $2,050 £1,025

Jumeau phonograph doll. $2,400 £1,200

A fine French automaton of a negro musician from the third quarter of the 19th century, 3ft. high. $3,300 £1,650

ACCORDIONS

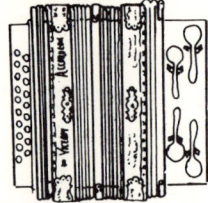

'The Viceroy', accordion complete with case. $60 £30

French accordion with mother-of-pearl keys, 7in. wide when closed. $140 £70

AMERICAN FIDDLE

American fiddle by Sylvanus J. Talbott, New Hampshire, circa 1887, total length 23¼in. $1,440 £720

BAGPIPES

A good stand of Great Highland Pipes by James Robertson, Edinburgh, with tartan bag cover. $450 £225

Edinburgh made set of bagpipes with the Gordon tartan. $500 £250

BANJOS

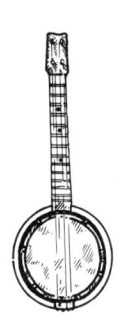

Small stained wood banjo with vellum head. $60 £30

An old 'Windsor' banjo. $70 £35

Early banjo, vellum head with six brass tensioners, 35¾in. long. $80 £40

Victorian banjo 'The Broadcaster'. $90 £45

Banjo with vellum head having forty tensioners and ivory turning pegs, 37in. long. $100 £50

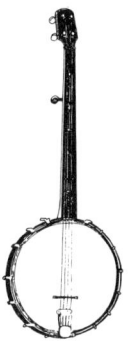

A fine banjo, with ebony faced stem, and brass drum body, in carrying case. $110 £55

11

BARREL ORGANS

Small table barrel organ. $380 £190

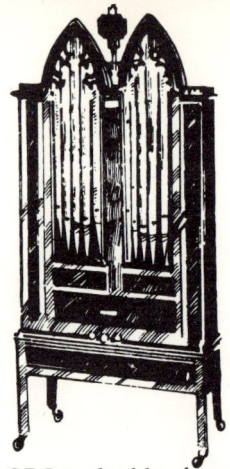

A C.T. Bates church barrel organ playing ten hymns, circa 1840, 5ft.9in. $770 £385

A mid 19th century miniature chamber barrel organ. $840 £420

Coin in slot barrel piano playing ten dance tunes, in a birchwood case. $1,110 £550

BARREL ORGANS

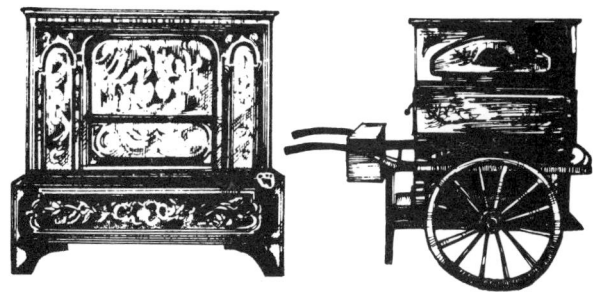

A rare Gavioli marquetry table barrel organ, 2ft.2in. wide, circa 1870. $1,480 £740

19th century ten air barrel organ by Keith Prowse & Co. London.
$2,020 £1,010

Late 18th century French barrel organ with painted panel, 25¾in. long. $2,460 £1,230

A beautifully inlaid street barrel organ, with a playing rank of piccolo pipes to the front.
$3,300 £1,650

BOWS

Silver mounted violin bow by W.E. Hill & Sons. $360 £180

Silver and tortoiseshell mounted violin bow by Paul Weidhaas, Markneukirchen, 20th century, 54gm. $380 £190

An unusual carved viola da gamba bow, probably English, 27in. long, 64gm. $410 £205

Silver and ivory mounted violin bow, 62gm, length 26in. $530 £265

Late 18th century ebony mounted violin bow by John Dodd, 51gm. $720 £360

Gold and tortoiseshell mounted violin bow by Malcolm M. Taylor, 65gm. $770 £385

English ivory mounted violin bow, 1776, 50gm., 30in. long. $820 £410

Silver mounted violin bow by W.E. Hill & Sons, London, 1944, 58gm. $960 £480

Gold mounted violin bow by Frans Winkler with gold mounted ebony frog, 55gm. $960 £480

BOWS

Fine gold and ivory mounted violin bow by J.S. Finkel, Swiss, 64gm. $960 £480

Silver mounted violin bow by Eugene Sartory, Paris, 55gm.
$1,010 £505

Silver and ivory mounted violoncello bow by W.E. Hill & Sons, 75gm. $1,150 £575

Silver and tortoiseshell mounted violin bow by W.E. Hill & Sons, 58gm. $1,200 £600

Silver mounted violin bow by Eury, Paris, 62gm. $1,250 £625

Silver mounted viola bow by E. Sartory, Paris, 63gm. $1,320 £660

19th century silver mounted violin bow by Nicolas Maire, 61gm. $1,320 £660

Gold and tortoiseshell violin bow by Emile Francois Ouchard, 64gm. $1,380 £690

Silver mounted violin bow by James Tubbs, London, 58gm.
$1,440 £720

BOWS

Gold mounted violin bow by Pierre Vidoudez, Geneva, 60gm.
$1,440 £720

Gold and ivory mounted violin bow by Dodd, 29in. long, 51gm.
$1,480 £740

Silver mounted violin bow by Victor Fetique, Paris, 62gm.
$1,480 £740

Gold and ivory mounted violin bow by E. Ouchard, 62gm.
$1,480 £740

Silver mounted violin bow by Eugene Sartory, Paris, 57gm.
$1,480 £740

French violin bow by the Peccatte family, 58gm.
$1,500 £750

A silver mounted violoncello bow by Eugene Sartory of Paris, 80gm.
$1,600 £800

Silver and ivory mounted violin bow by Eugene Sartory, Paris.
$1,680 £840

Fine silver mounted violin bow by James Tubbs, London, 59gm.
$1,870 £935

Gold and tortoiseshell mounted violin bow by W.E. Hill & Sons, London, 59gm. $1,880 £940

A gold mounted viola bow by W. E. Hill & Sons, the octagonal stick of Pernambuco, 65gm. $1,900 £950

Silver and tortoiseshell violoncello bow by W E. Hill & Sons, 80gm. $1,920 £960

Silver mounted violin bow by James Tubbs, 60gm.
$1,960 £980

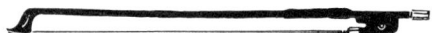

Silver mounted violoncello bow by Eugene Sartory, Paris, 84gm. $2,100 £1,050

A chased gold mounted violoncello bow by W. E. Hill & Sons, 85gm. $2,100 £1,050

Fine silver mounted violin bow by Simon Pageot, Mirecourt, 56gm. $2,100 £1,050

Early 19th century gold mounted violin bow by Jacques Lafleur, Paris, 57gm. $2,400 £1,200

Gold and tortoiseshell mounted violin bow by W.E. Hill & Sons, 58gm. $2,400 £1,200

BOWS

Silver mounted violin bow by Francois Tourte, 55gm. $2,400 £1,200

Early 19th century silver mounted violin bow by John Dodd, 64gm. $2,600 £1,300

Gold mounted violin bow by Georges Mougenot, Brussels, circa 1875, 66gm. $2,640 £1,320

Silver mounted viola bow by James Tubbs, London, 72gm. $3,200 £1,600

Gold mounted violin bow by James Tubbs, 65gm. $3,300 £1,650

A chased gold mounted violin bow by W. E. Hill & Sons, 59gm. $3,300 £1,650

Early 19th century gold and ivory mounted violin bow, 61gm, by John Dodd. $3,520 £1,760

French gold and ivory mounted violin bow by Eugene Sartory, Paris, 66gm. $3,520 £1,760

Gold mounted violin bow by Francois Tourte, 60gm. $5,940 £2,970

BUGLES

A Victorian brass bugle. $30 £15

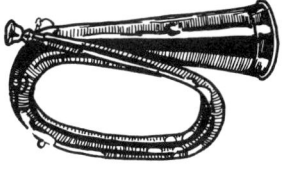

19th century copper bugle with brass embellishments. $40 £20

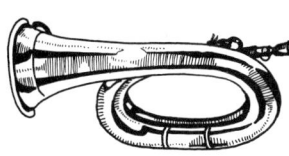

A Victorian silver plated bugle. $50 £25

Keyed bugle by Clementi & Co., 18in. long, circa 1820. $140 £70

A rare Nazi S.A. bugle, with brass and German silver mounted N.S.D.A.P. eagle at mouthpiece, fitted with additional extension. $180 £90

A bugle and sword carried at Waterloo by Lord Gantley. $840 £420

CECILIUM

Mid 19th century Cecilium by Arthur Quentin de Gromard, Paris. 4ft. 1½in. high. $720 £360

CETERONE

Ceterone by Robert Hadaway, Norfolk, 1970, 61¾in. long, in fitted case. $670 £335

CELLOS

A cello and bow in canvas case. $200 £100

19th century cello by Jules Remy of Paris. $1,080 £540

A fine cello by George Panomo, London, circa 1830. $12,000 £6,000

CHITARRONE

COR ANGLAIS

Italian composite Chitarrone labelled Michele Atton, 1610, 79½in. long. $720 £360

A curved Cor Anglais by Triebert of Paris, 30¾ in. long, circa 1850.
$3,000 £1,500

CORNETS

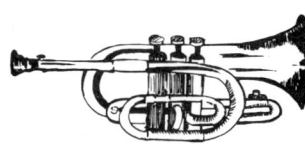

Brass cornet with mother-of-pearl keys. $70 £35

Small cornet, by Boosey & Co., London, circa 1880, 7½in. long.
$360 £200

Silver plated cornet by Antoine Courtois, 1862, in original mahogany case. $640 £320

21

CLARINETS

A boxwood and ivory mounted clarinet by Golding & Co., of London. circa 1800. $120 £60

A fine boxwood thirteen key clarinet, by Buffet, Crampion & Co., Paris. $180 £90

Eight-keyed boxwood clarinet by D'Almaine & Co., London, circa 1850, 23in. long. $198 £110

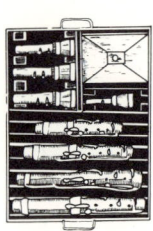 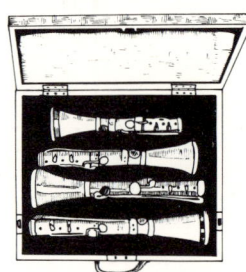

Rare set of four clarinets by Richard John Bolton, London, circa 1840. $2,420 £1,210

Important five keyed boxwood clarinet by Henry Kusder, London, circa 1865, 26¼in. long. $5,720 £2,860

CLAVICHORDS

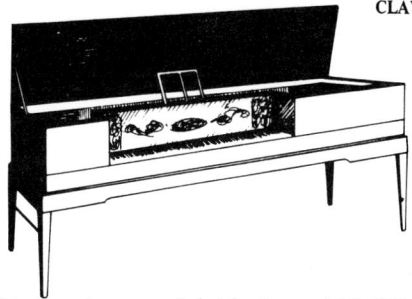

A Victorian mahogany cased clavichord. $380 £190

Late 18th century German clavichord in a walnut case, 36½in. long.
$3,450 £1,725

German Gebunden clavichord by George Friedrich Schmahl, Ulm, 1807, 54in. wide. $5,000 £2,500

CORNOPEAN

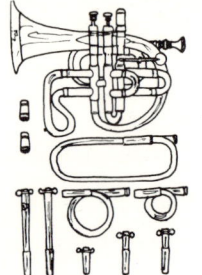

A cornopean by F. Pace, Westminster, circa 1835. $650 £325

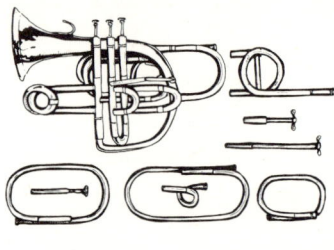

Good cornopean in wooden box, by Thomas Key, London. $670 £335

Mid 19th century brass cornopean by H. Kohler, London, 13in. long. $840 £420

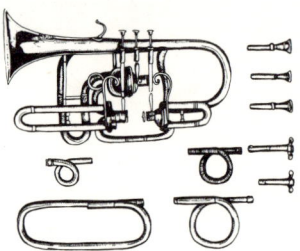

Brass cornopean by Henry Kohler, London, mid 19th century. $1,010 £505

COUENOPHONE

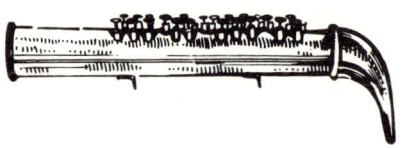

Late 19th century Couenophone, 17½in. long, Paris. $162 £90

DRUMS

18th century military sidedrum by Robert Horne, 12in. diameter.
$60 £30

A Victorian sidedrum. $80 £40

A rare Georgian copper kettle drum of the Honourable East India Company, 19in. diam., 19in. high.
$130 £65

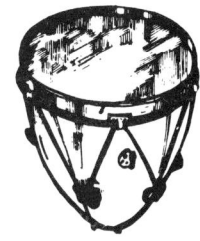

An early 19th century military tambour, with all-brass shell.
$140 £70

A fine early 19th century military tambour, having all-brass shell with cords to brass securing rim holding skin. $160 £80

Military painted drum of the Hampshire Regiment, 14½in. high.
$160 £80

DRUMS

Royal Scots 4th/5th Battalion
(Queen's Edinburgh) drum. $180 £90

A rare Georgian military bass drum, painted with post - 1838 Royal Arms motto and foliage, 25in. diam., 31in. long. $260 £130

A large Georgian military drum with wooden frame, 20½in. diam. $260 £130

Small sidedrum signed Thomas Emblin, 1776, with two pipes. $300 £150

Shaman's drum from the North-West Pacific coast. $820 £410

One of a pair of Thai bronze drums, 48cm. high. $1,730 £865

ESRAR **EUPHONIUM** **FAGOTTINO**

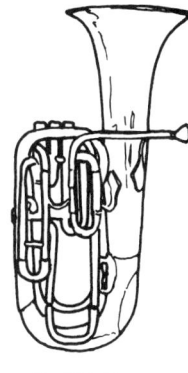

An Indian esrar from the early 19th century. $190 £95

French brass euphonium. $120 £60

Late 18th century miniature fagottino 27in. long. $306 £170

FLAGEOLET

Six-keyed rosewood flageolet by Monzani, London, circa 1815, total length 21½in. $220 £110

Boxwood and ivory mounted double flageolet by Clementi & Co., circa 1810. $620 £310

Boxwood double flageolet by William Bainbridge, London, 19½in. long, circa 1827. $756 £420

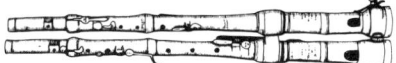

Rare boxwood double flute flageolet by Wm. Bainbridge, London, 23½in. long, circa 1830. $1,010 £505

FLUTES

Blackman flute in case. $80 £40

Eleven keyed rosewood flute by Henry Hill, 28¼in. long. $290 £145

Fine six keyed boxwood flute by Clementi & Co., London, circa 1810. $460 £230

Boxwood four-keyed flute by Rudall & Rose, London, 1840-50, 21in. long. $432 £240

One keyed boxwood flute by William Millhouse, 21¼in. long, circa 1790. $520 £260

Carved ivory six keyed flute by Henry Hill, London, 23¼in. long. $650 £325

Fine eight keyed ivory flute by Louis Drouet, London, circa 1815, sounding length 23½in., in leather case. $820 £410

Good one keyed stained boxwood flute by Thomas Cahusac, London, late 18th century, 21in. long. $910 £455

A fine eight keyed ivory flute by Louis Drouet of London, circa 1815. $1,010 £505

FLUTES

Late 18th century four-keyed flute, 21in. long.
$1,206 £670

Ten keyed ivory flute by Henry Hill, London, circa 1835, 24½in. long.
$1,870 £935

French one keyed ivory flute, mid 18th century, sounding length 21½in., unstamped. $1,920 £960

One keyed boxwood flute by Proser, London, late 18th century, 21¼in. long. $2,040 £1,020

Important one keyed flute by Thomas Stanesby Junior, London, 1738. $2,640 £1,320

Maori bone flute, carved with a grotesque tiki-like figure. $3,520 £1,760

Mid 18th century one-keyed boxwood flute, 21¾in. long. $6,120 £3,400

An important gold mounted ivory concert flute by Thomas Stanesby Junior, London, circa 1740. $8,800 £4,400

An important two keyed flute in its original case, formerly the property of Frederick The Great of Prussia. $12,760 £6,380

GRAMOPHONES

Pixie Grippa portable gramophone.
$30 £15

Edwardian mahogany cased record player. $40 £20

E.M. Ginn Expert Senior 'Oversize' gramophone. $70 £35

English maxitone portable gramophone, circa 1925-35, 10in. turntable. $180 £90

A Beltona square gramophone with chromium plated horn. $180 £90

Late 19th century gramophone with a fine brass horn. $190 £95

GRAMOPHONES

French Pathe portable gramophone with 28cm. turntable, circa 1925-35. $200 £100

Edwardian table gramophone with metal horn. $220 £110

An early gramophone with a fine brass horn. $240 £120

An E.M.G. Mark 10B gramophone with a papier mache horn. $240 £120

Columbia model AA gramophone with two-minute gearing, American circa 1902-1904. $290 £145

His Master's Voice Horn gramophone, circa 1915. $310 £155

GRAMOPHONES

Zonophone gramophone with 12in. turntable, 1ft.3½in., English, dated 6.2.20. $360 £180

Edison Bell discaphone gramophone, English circa 1910-1920. $360 £180

Duophone table console gramophone with twin sound boxes, English circa 1924. $360 £180

Gramophone Company horn gramophone with Zonophone sound box, English circa 1904. $360 £180

An Edison Bell 'Domestic A' gramophone by Pathe Freres, circa 1901. $380 £190

An interesting bugle-twist horn gramophone, 39in. high. $390 £195

GRAMOPHONES

Gramophone Company gramophone lacks winding handle, English circa 1905-1910. $430 £215

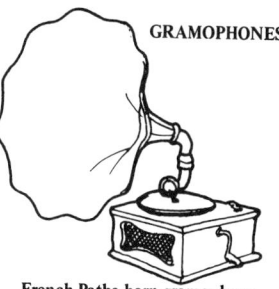

French Pathe horn gramophone, circa 1910-1920, with 11in. turntable. $480 £240

Gramophone and Typewriter Ltd. double spring Monarch gramophone, 1ft.10in., English circa 1904. $480 £240

Gramophone Company intermediate Monarch gramophone with 10in. turntable, English dated Jan 1917. $530 £265

Gramophone Company Junior Monarch gramophone, 1ft.6in., English circa 1910. $530 £265

H.M.V. 'Lumiere' gramophone in oak case, 1ft.4½in. x 1ft.11in., 1924-25. $540 £270

GRAMOPHONES

E.M.G. mark 1XB gramophone with papier mache horn, 1ft.9in., English circa 1930. $580 £290

An Apollo gramophone with 9in. turntable, English circa 1910. $620 £310

H.M.V. model 460 gramophone with 12in. turntable, Lumiere pleated paper diaphragm, English circa 1924. $650 £325

French Pathe horn gramophone, circa 1910-1915. $820 £410

English H.M.V. gramophone with Lumiere pleated paper diaphragm, in an oak box with hinged lid, circa 1925. $820 £410

Gramophone Company Limited trade mark gramophone, 7in. turntable, English, 1902. $890 £445

GRAMOPHONES

A Parlophone coin-in-slot gramophone in beechwood case with 'Reform-type' sound box, 22½in. x 18in., date on base 6.12.15. $890 £445

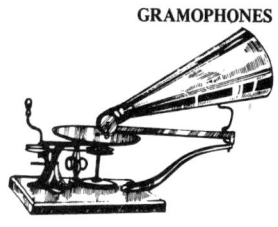

A Gramophone Company hand driven style No. 2 gramophone with 7in. diameter turntable, 1898-1901. $1,250 £625

A rare Columbia gramophone which plays both 5in. and 2in. diameter cylinders, circa 1900. $1,920 £960

Rare German hand driven gramophone by Kammerer and Reinhardt, 1890-95. $2,280 £1,140

Berliner gramophone by Kammerer and Reinhardt of Waltershausen, Germany, circa 1890. $2,500 £1,250

A hand driven Berliner gramophone. $2,500 £1,250

GUITARS

Italian guitar labelled Guiseppe Soiale, Via Del Cordo, Nig, Roma, 1838, 17½in. long. $120 £60

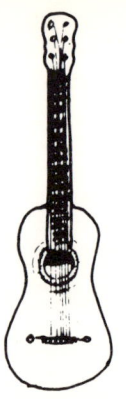

Guitar labelled Louis Panormo, London, 17½in. long. $150 £75

English guitar or cittern by William Prior, 1727, length of back 13¼in. $360 £180

English guitar or cittern by Michael Rauche, London 1768, length of back 13½in. $430 £215

English guitar or cittern by Michael Rauche, London 1766, length of back, 13½in. $430 £215

Late 18th century English guitar or cittern by John Preston, London, length of back 13½in. $480 £240

GUITARS

An Italian steel string guitar by Mario Maccaferri. $600 £300

An Italian guitar by Gennard Fabricatore, Naples, 1817. $640 £320

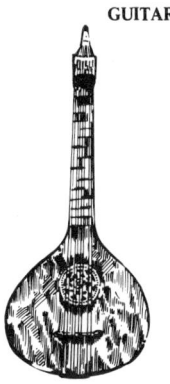

Late 18th. century English guitar by John Preston, London, 14in. long. $1,116 £620

Late 18th century English keyed guitar or cittern, length 28¾in. $1,680 £840

18th century Italian guitar, 36in. long. $4,160 £2,080

Pine, rosewood and fruitwood guitar by Matheus Evv, 1643. $4,500 £2,500

GUITARS

18th century
French guitar,
37in. long.
$6,470 £3,235

Chitarra Battente
signed on the head
Andreas Ott,
Prague, 37in. long.
$8,000 £4,000

18th century
Italian guitar,
36in. long.
$8,000 £4,000

HARMONICOR

Late 19th. century Harmonicor, made in Paris,
19in. long. $198 £110

An interesting mid 19th. century Harmonicor by
Louis Jules Jaulin, Paris, 19½in. long. $500 £250

HARMONIUM   HARMONIUM

Mid 19th century portatine harmonium by A. F. Debain, 2ft. 1in. high, on a tripod support with foot pedal at base. $500 £250

HARPS

Inlaid table harp, circa 1815. $280 £140

19th century harp by Erard. $370 £185

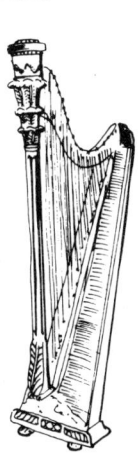

French giltwood harp by Renault, circa 1775. $600 £300

HARPS

A North Italian hook harp, dated 1776, 67in. high. $620 £310

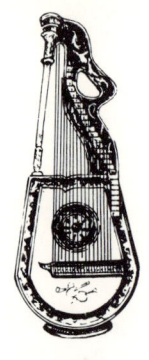

Early 19th century Dutch harp by Edward Light. $660 £330

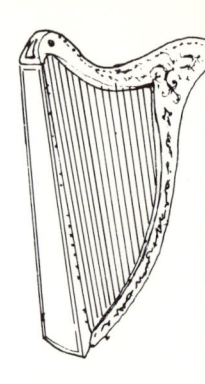

Irish 'Royal Portable' harp, signed J. Egan, Dublin, 35in. high. $670 £335

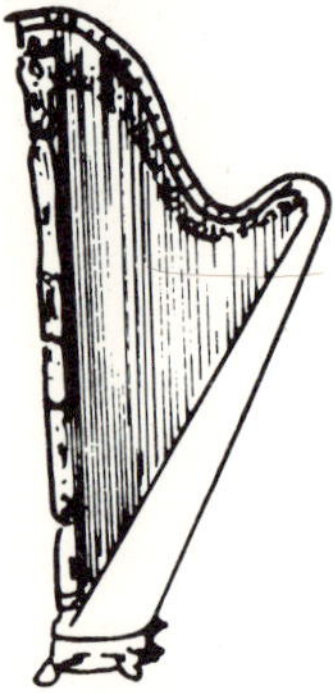

Grecian double action harp, signed on the neck Erard's Patent Harp, 66½in. high. $670 £335

Attractive Dital harp by Edward Light, London, the simulated rosewood body in seven sections, circa 1815, 34½in. high. $910 £455

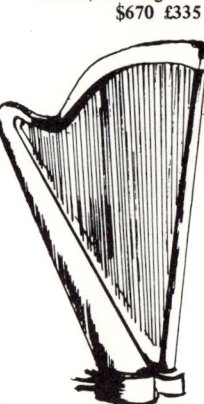

Early 19th century harp by Sebastion Svard, 5ft.6in. high. $1,010 £505

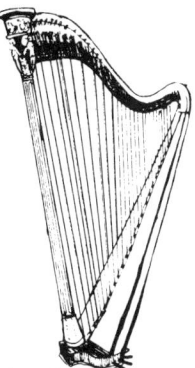

HARPS

An early 19th century harp, with carved figures of Athenians and fluted in Empire style, with eight pedals, by Sebastion Erard, 5ft.6in. high. $1,080 £540

19th century English pedal harp by Erard, London, 5ft. 9½in. high. $1,440 £720

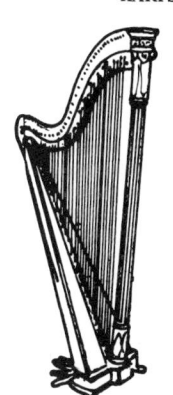

A single action harp by Erard Freres of Paris, circa 1790. $1,960 £980

French pedal harp by Cousineau, Paris, circa 1775, 5ft.3¾in. high. $2,040 £1,020

Late 18th century small single action harp, French, with seven pedals, 5ft. 1in. high. $2,160 £1,080

French pedal harp by Cousineau, Paris, circa 1770, 5ft.4½in. high. $3,300 £1,650

41

HARPSICHORDS

Late 19th century Italian octave harpsichord on an oak frame, 19in. wide. $1,870 £935

Two-manual harpsichord by Henry Tull, London, 3ft.4¼in. wide. $3,520 £1,760

A fine two-manual harpsichord by Jacob Kirckman, London 1767. $13,200 £6,600

Fine two-manual harpsichord by Jacob and Abraham Kirckman, London 1783, in a mahogany case, 3ft.1¾in. wide. $15,400 £7,700

HARPSICHORDS

A two-manual harpsichord in an inlaid marquetry case by Jacob Kirckman, circa 1755. $18,700 £9,350

American two-manual harpsichord by Charles Trute & Weidberg, Philadelphia, 1794, 7ft. 8½in. long. $20,600 £10,300

Flemish two-manual harpsichord by Hans the Younger, the sound board painted with Apollo and the nine muses, circa 1690. $21,000 £10,500

Superb harpsichord by Jean Antoine Vaudry, 1681. $40,000 £20,000

HORNS

Copper and brass coaching horn, circa 1870, 4½in. diameter. $90 £45

A silver plated nickle hunting horn, with elegant solid silver shield, hallmarked for Birmingham, 9in. long. $80 £40

Silver hunting horn, 1923. $90 £45

A copper coaching horn with brass centre band and mouth piece by Harris & Nixon, circa 1840, 41½in. long. $120 £60

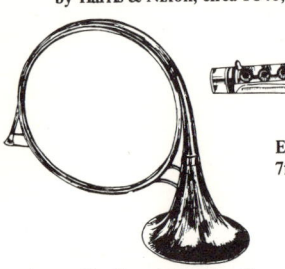

English brass horn, circa 1800, 7ft.3in. long. $600 £300

A very fine French brass hunting horn. $300 £150

A fine and rare late 17th century English boxwood hunting horn. $1,020 £510

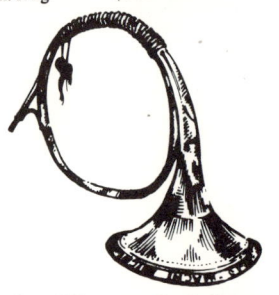

Late 17th century Cor de Chasse, 165½in. long. $684 £380

HORNS

Late 19th century Faience model horn decorated in green, orange and blue on a white ground, probably French. $1,250 £625

Hunting horn made by Phipps and Robinson, London 1792. $1,380 £690

A rare French horn by John Christopher Hofmaster of London, circa 1710. $1,800 £900

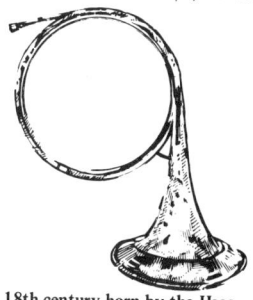

18th century horn by the Haas family of Nuremberg, 149½in. long. $2,000 £1,000

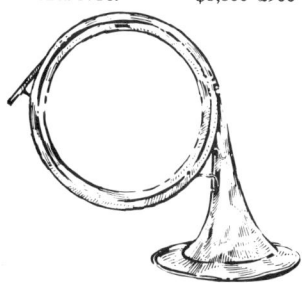

A horn in 'D' engraved on the garland 'Iohann Wilhelm Haas in Nuremberg', 186in. long, early 18th century. $2,000 £1,000

One of a pair of silver hunting horns made in Vienna in 1775. $20,000 £10,000

HURDY GURDIES

French hurdy gurdy by Caron, Versailles, circa 1770, with S-shaped iron handle, 26in. long. $1,580 £790

Mid 18th century fine small hurdy gurdy in leather bound case, 14¼in. long. $2,160 £1,080

KITS

Late 18th century kit by Henry Jay, London, length of back 8½in. $1,320 £660

Mid 18th century English dancing master's kit, 15¾in. long, sold with bow. $1,740 £870

LUTES

Lute labelled Joachim Tielke, Hamburg, 1748, 40¾in. long. $280 £140

Fine thirteen-course baroque lute by Thomas Goff and J.C. Cobby, London 1955, length of body 21in. $960 £480

LYRES

LYRES

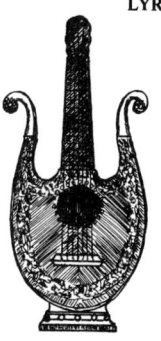

Mahogany box lyre with fifteen strings, 27 in. high. $100 £50

Teak wood and copper banded Whalingman's lyre, circa 1850, the side supports carved as dolphins, 23in. high. $120 £60

A lyre guitar by Harley, London circa 1810, 34 in. high. $700 £350

MANDORAS

Milanese mandora, signed Antonio Stradivari, Cremona, circa 1700, 20in. long. $480 £240

Early 18th century mandora, unlabelled, length of body 11½in. $770 £385

Late 17th century Italian mandora inlaid with mother-of-pearl and tortoiseshell, 22in. long. $3,340 £1,680

MANDOLINS

A mandolin, the table decorated with mother-of-pearl flowers and banding, in carrying case. $80 £40

Mandolin labelled Stridente Fabrica Di Mandolini, Via Antonion, Napoli, 24in. long. $90 £45

A finely inlaid late 19th century mandolin by Strident, Naples. $120 £60

19th century English miniature mandolin overlaid with tortoiseshell, 5in. long. $130 £65

Late 18th century Neapolitan mandolin by Joao Vieira da Silva, Lisbon, total length 23¼in. $670 £335

Mandolin by Antonio Vinaccia, Naples, 1774, 11in. high. $864 £480

MUSIC STANDS

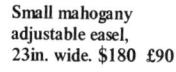

Small mahogany adjustable easel, 23in. wide. $180 £90

Victorian mahogany music stand, 11in. wide. $310 £155

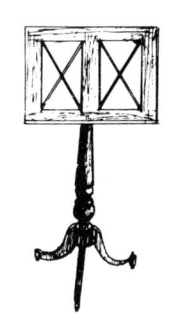

19th century mahogany music stand on turned pillar and fluted tripod feet, with a brass candle bracket, 3ft.6in. high. $320 £160

Mid 19th century William IV mahogany music stand, 17½in. wide. $720 £360

Regency rosewood music stand with reeded legs. $840 £420

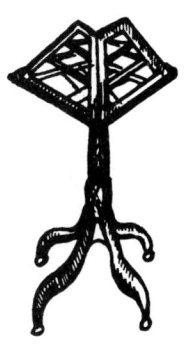

18th century mahogany music stand. $900 £450

MISCELLANEOUS

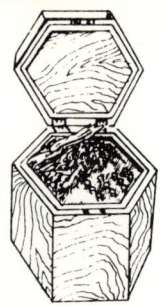

Victorian concertina, complete with case. $40 £20

Victorian metronome in an oak case. $40 £20

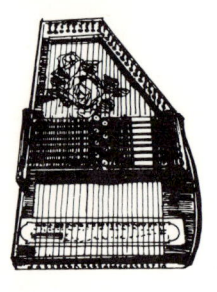

19th century autoharp, with floral decoration. $72 £36

A rare and interesting American radio in the form of a Coca Cola bottle, 24in. high, circa 1930. $360 £180

Native string instrument with hide and shell ornament. $30 £15

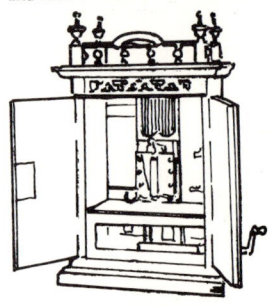

Edwardian smoker's cabinet Alexandra disc musical box. $1,240 £620

MISCELLANEOUS

Late 18th century set of eight tuning forks in case. $378 £210

19th century metronome in a figured walnut case, by R. Cocks and Co., London, 9½in. high. $116 £58

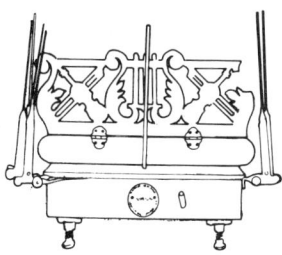

Late 19th century Padbury's patent 'Indispensable' music leaf turner, 9in. wide. $160 £80

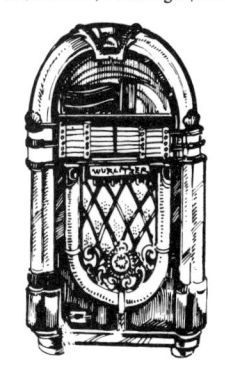

Wurlitzer juke box with twenty-four records, 1946. $3,800 £1,900

'Nipper' a plaster advertising model of a dog for H.M.V. $530 £265

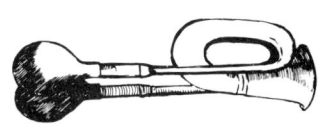

Edwardian brass car horn, with two notes. $54 £27

51

MUSICAL BOXES

A Swiss musical box in a rosewood inlaid case. $150 £75

Victorian music box shaped as a mandolin, in tortoiseshell and mother-of-pearl, complete with strings. $150 £75

Mahogany inlaid music box with one drum, 14½in. wide. $190 £95

Victorian music box in a walnut case, playing eight airs. $270 £135

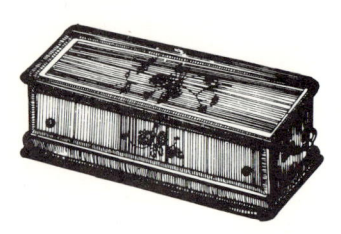

19th century musical box playing eight airs, Paris 1878. $270 £135

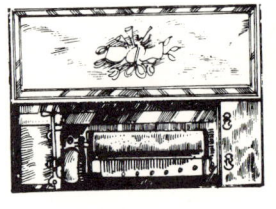

Late 19th century Swiss cylinder musical box playing ten airs, 1ft. 9in. wide. $290 £145

MUSICAL BOXES

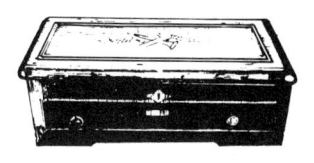

A Swiss musical box with three bells, in a rosewood inlaid and banded case, 16½in. long. $300 £150

A 19th century, Swiss musical box, in rosewood inlaid case, 18in. wide. $320 £160

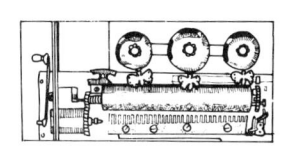

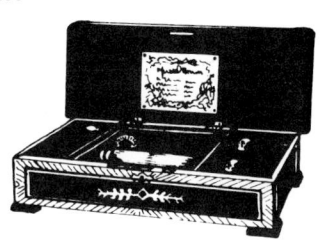

B.H. Abrahams 'Bells in Sight' cylinder musical box, 38cm. wide, Swiss late 19th century. $360 £180

19th century Swiss musical box in a rosewood case inlaid with birds and fruit. $390 £185

Late 19th century Swiss 'Bells in Sight' cylinder musical box, 1ft.7in. wide. $400 £200

German 9½in. Kallippe disc musical box, 11½in. wide, with twelve discs, circa 1905. $530 £265

MUSICAL BOXES

Swiss key wound cylinder musical box, 1ft. wide, circa 1850. $580 £290

Mid 19th century Swiss made music box with brass inlaid lid, the key wind movement playing twelve operatic airs. $600 £300

Small oblong musical box edged in gilt and mounted with 'Rose Pampadour' enamel panels, with singing bird. $600 £300

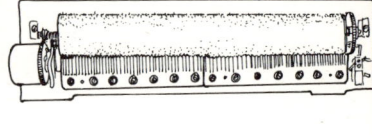

Swiss cylinder musical box by Nicole Freres, circa 1875. $620 £310

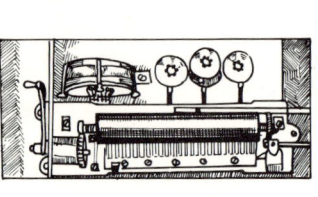

Late 19th century Swiss 'Bells and Drum in Sight' cylinder musical box, 1ft.8in. wide. $620 £310

Late 19th century Swiss three cylinder musical box on stand, 3ft.5in. wide. $650 £325

MUSICAL BOXES

A Swiss musical box with ten airs, in rosewood inlaid and ebonised case, 22in. **$770 £385**

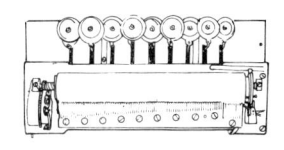

Swiss, late 19th century 'Bells in Sight' cylinder musical box, 2ft.2in. wide. **$770 £385**

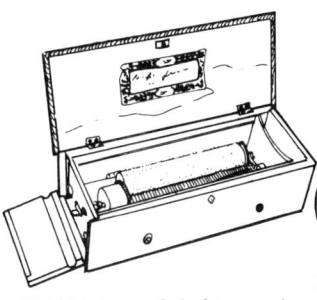

Mid 19th century Swiss key wound cylinder musical box in a rosewood case and reeded edged lid, 1ft.3in. wide. **$770 £385**

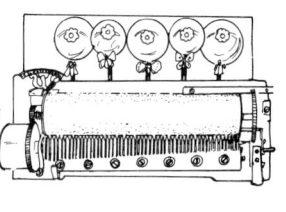

Late 19th century Swiss 'Bells in Sight' cylinder musical box, 1ft.11in. wide, in simulated rosewood case. **$770 £385**

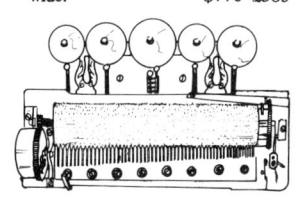

Late 19th century Swiss 'Bells in Sight' cylinder musical box in a rosewood case with fruitwood floral design, 1ft.9in. wide. **$770 £385**

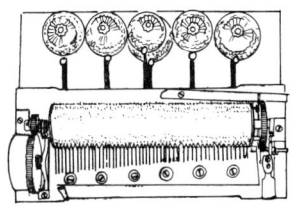

Late 19th century Swiss 'Bells in Sight' cylinder musical box which plays ten tunes, 1ft.10in. wide. **$820 £410**

MUSICAL BOXES

A Victorian 'Penny in the Slot' walnut musical cabinet in the form of a theatre. $900 £450

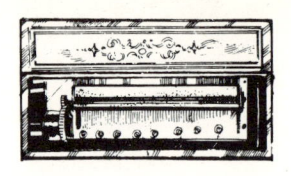

A Nicole Freres key wound cylinder musical box, 1ft.6in. wide, Swiss, circa 1900. $960 £480

Swiss late 19th century upright cylinder musical box, 2ft.2in. wide. $960 £480

19th century Swiss musical box in a rosewood case. $960 £480

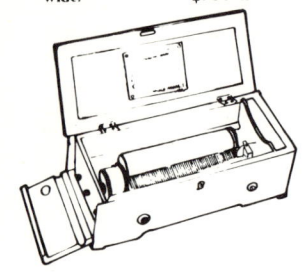

Nicole Freres cylinder musical box, Swiss, circa 1842, 1ft.3in. wide. $1,010 £505

Good Nicole Freres key wound cylinder musical box, 1ft.2in. wide, Swiss, circa 1840. $1,060 £530

MUSICAL BOXES

Victorian musical box by Robert F. Knoeloch of Bremerhaven with timepiece which operates the musical action every hour. $1,080 £540

19th century Swiss musical box complete with a miniature turbanned drummer sitting amongst the works, in a rosewood case. $1,140 £570

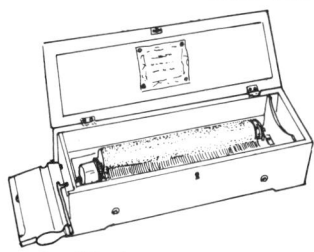

Good Nicole Freres hand wound cylinder musical box, circa 1860, 1ft.8in. wide. $1,150 £575

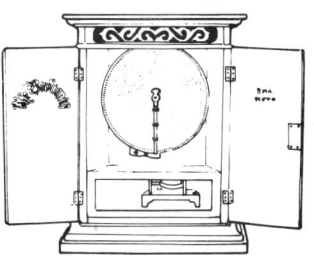

Swiss 11½in. Britannia disc musical box, 2ft. high, with nine metal discs, circa 1905. $1,150 £575

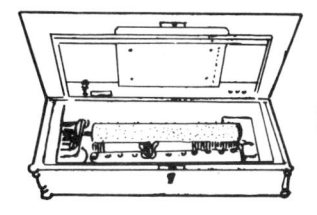

Unusual Harp-Mandolin-Picole cylinder musical box, 17in. wide, by Bremond and Greiner. $1,200 £600

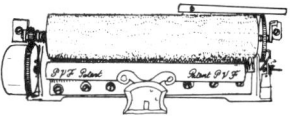

Good Paillard, Vaucher, Fils, 'mandolin' cylinder musical box, 1ft.8in. wide, Swiss, late 19th century. $1,200 £600

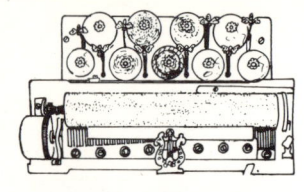

MUSICAL BOXES

Late 19th century Swiss 'Bells in Sight' cylinder musical box in a rosewood case, 2ft.2in. wide. $1,220 £610

Swiss Mojon, Manger & Co., cylinder musical box, 2ft.8in. wide, circa 1880. $1,250 £625

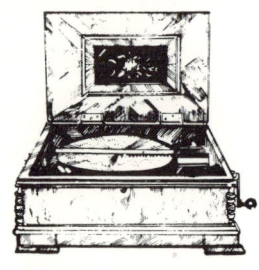

A large German Stella disc musical box with six discs of 17¼in. diam. circa 1900. $1,250 £625

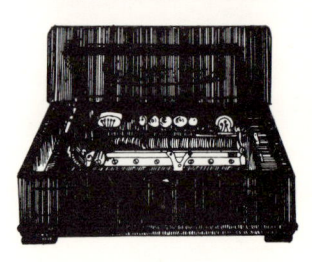

19th century French musical box in burr yew wood and ebonised case, 24in. wide. $1,320 £660*

A Swiss organ musical box playing six airs, 66cm. wide. $1,350 £675

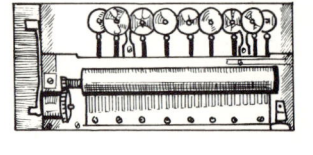

Swiss Bremond 'Bells in Sight' cylinder musical box, 1ft.11in. wide, circa 1880. $1,390 £695

MUSICAL BOXES

19th century musical box with four interchangeable cylinders. $1,400 £700

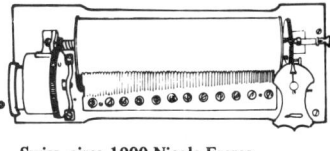

Swiss, circa 1900 Nicole Freres cylinder musical box. $1,530 £765

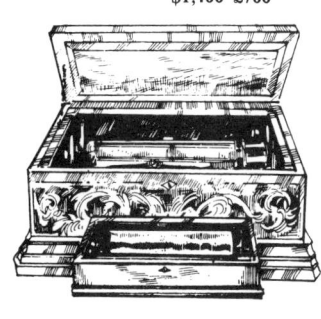

A Mermond Freres interchangeable cylinder musical box with four cylinders, 3ft.3in. wide. $1,920 £960

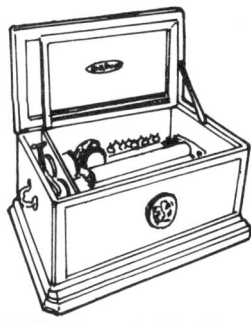

Late Victorian musical chest in burr walnut and ebonised case, patent K. Prowse & Co., London. $2,120 £1,060

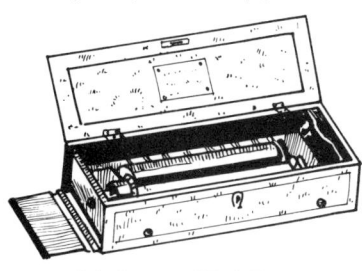

Swiss keywound Nicole Freres cylinder musical box, 1ft.8in. wide, circa 1841. $2,210 £1,105

Swiss musical box in a walnut and kingwood banded case on a table stand with ebonised and turned legs. $2,280 £1,140

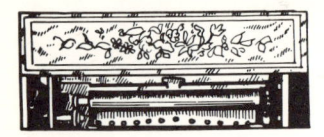

MUSICAL BOXES

Good Nicole Freres pianoforte cylinder musical box, Swiss, circa 1881, 2ft.4in. wide. $2,400 £1,200

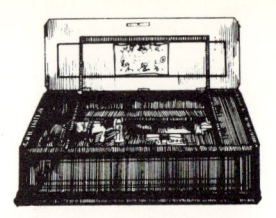

19th century Swiss musical box in a burr walnut case crossbanded with ebony, 3ft.11in. wide. $2,400 £1,200

A Victorian musical box, set on a table with extra cylinders in the drawer. $3,080 £1,540

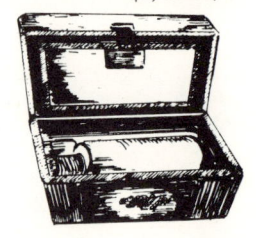

A fine musical box by Nicole Freres. $3,300 £1,650

A superb Stella disc musical box, circa 1901. $5,600 £2,800

Swiss flute basse, voix celeste, interchangeable cylinder musical box by Langdorff et Fils, circa 1850. $9,000 £5,000

OBOES   OBOES

Stained boxwood ten-keyed oboe, 22¼in. long, circa 1860. $153 £85

An early 19th century oboe from Nigeria, 17in. long. $190 £95

Early 19th century Tibetan oboe of wood body with brass bell, 17in. long.
$200 £100

A two-keyed late 18th century stained boxwood oboe, by George Astor, London.
$1,730 £865

A tenor oboe by T. Cahusac, third quarter of 18th century. $2,600 £1,300

Rare ivory three-keyed oboe by Klenig, mid 18th century, 22¾in. long.
$7,400 £3,700

Late 17th century three-keyed baroque oboe, by Thomas Stanesby senior, London.
$7,800 £3,900

OCARINA

Early 20th century ceramic Ocarina by Meissen, 7¾in. long. $90 £50

Early 20th century Ocarina by Meissen, 7¼in. long. $99 £55

Early 20th century Ocarina by Meissen, 7¾in. long. $135 £75

OCTAVINO

17th century Italian octavino in cypress case on oak Regency style stand.
$3,040 £1,520

OPERAPHONE

Operaphone Gramophone, circa 1925-30, 3ft. high. $504 £280

OPHICLEIDES

Twelve-keyed copper ophicleide with crook and mouthpiece, circa 1840. $180 £90

Mid 19th century ophicleide, 41in. long. $270 £150

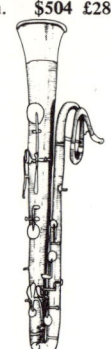

Mid 19th century ophicleide, total length 9ft. $860 £430

ORPHICA

Late 18th century Vienese orphica, 41in. long in a case bound with red velvet. $3,740 £1,870

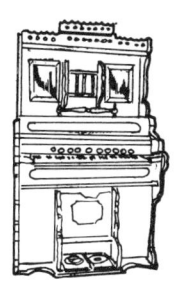

ORGANS

Mid Victorian carved oak organ.
$100 £50

19th century organ in a rosewood case, in working order. $180 £90

A very rare 19th century disc organette. $480 £240

An English 19th century 'Competition' pipe organ with sixty-one keys and twelve stops, 7ft. high. $930 £465

Late 18th century French bible organ, 17in. long, 13¼in. wide. $1,080 £540

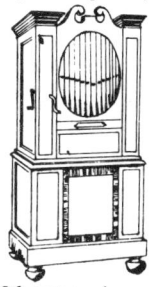

Late 18th century pipe organ operated by a handle at the side. $1,440 £720

ORGANS

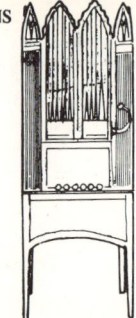

Regency mahogany mechanical organ, 24in. $1,920 £960

Mid 18th century Italian positive organ with hand operated bellows at the rear, 37in. wide. $4,620 £2,310

A superb chamber organ by Elliot, 1814. $14,500 £7,250

Late 18th century German positive organ on Regency style oak stand, 21in. wide. $3,040 £1,520

Fine Dutch chamber organ by T. Strumphler, Amsterdam, 1792, 43in. long. $5,940 £2,970

An enormous Imhof and Mukle orchestrion, 12ft.6in. high. $18,700 £9,350

PHONOGRAPHS

Edison Gem set on a green oak base, with handle wind, circa 1907. $110 £55

Columbia Phonograph graphophone Model 'Q' with rare open works and key wind, circa 1900. $120 £60

An Edison Bell standard phonograph with loud speaker. $130 £65

Edison standard phonograph, circa 1907. $180 £90

Britannia phonograph with key wound open mechanism, German circa 1903-1908. $200 £100

Edison standard phonograph complete with ten cylinder records. $200 £100

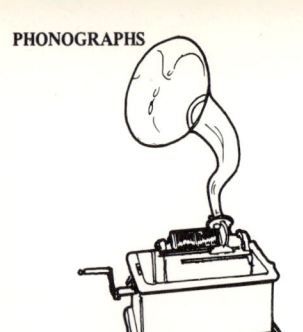

PHONOGRAPHS

Edison phonograph with metal horn. $210 £105

Thomas Edison phonograph, together with nineteen cylinders. $270 £135

Edison Bell Gem phonograph with New Model reproducer, English circa 1904-1908. $290 £145

Excelsior phonograph with two-minute gearing, German circa 1904-1908. $290 £145

An Edison Home phonograph cylinder player, with a Diamond 'B' reproducer and a magnificent signet horn, circa 1907. $290 £145

G.C. & Co. phonograph with Puck-type mechanism, German circa 1900-1905. $310 £155

PHONOGRAPHS

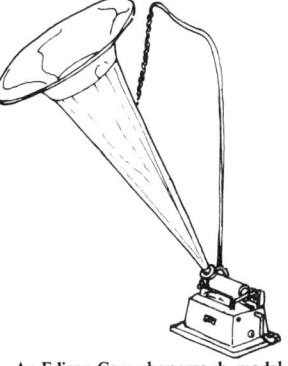

An Edison Gem phonograph, model 'C'. $310 £155

Pathe democratic phonograph, model No. 'O', French circa 1904. $340 £170

Reinhold & Co. Puck phonograph with conical nickel horn, German circa 1904-1908. $340 £170

Columbia Puck-type phonograph, model 'AQ', American circa 1900. $340 £170

Lyrophonwerke Koh-I-Noor Favourite phonograph, German circa 1908. $340 £170

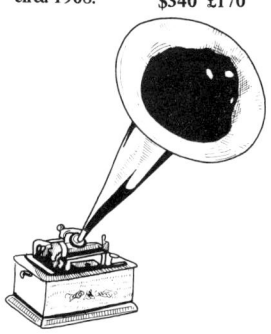

Edison Bell standard phonograph, 2ft.6in. high, English 1904-1908. $360 £180

PHONOGRAPHS

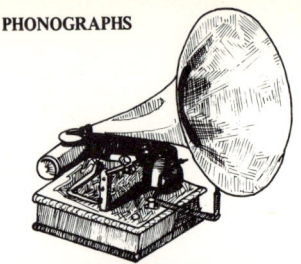

German G.C. & Co. phonograph with spun aluminium horn, circa 1900-1905. $360 £180

Good Lambertphone Entertainer phonograph, German circa 1904, lacks reproducer. $360 £180

Edison Home phonograph Model A. No. H1 24524 in green oak case, 1ft. 6in. long, circa 1901-04. $400 £200

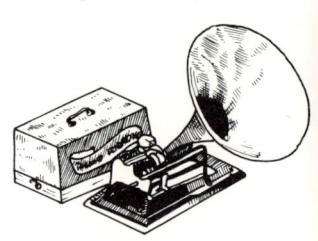

Swiss Paillards echophone phonograph, 12in. high, 30.5cm. diam. at mouth, circa 1905-1910. $410 £20

Edison Bell phonograph with two minute gearing and modern brass belled witches hat horn. $460 £230

American Edison Home phonograph, 1906-08. $460 £230

PHONOGRAPHS

Edison gem phonograph with two and four minute gearing, American 1905-1908. $500 £250

Edison Bell gem phonograph model D, American 1908-1912. $500 £250

Edison Home phonograph complete with horn and cylinders. $530 £265

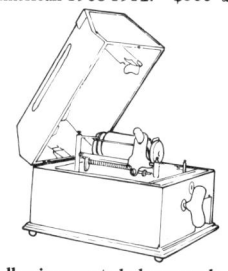

Small coin-operated phonograph, in an oak cabinet with hinged lid, possibly Continental, circa 1905-1910. $600 £300

An Edison phonograph with a particularly fine brass horn. $620 £310

Edison Home phonograph in a light oak case, American circa 1904. $650 £325

PHONOGRAPHS

A fine First World War Edison Bell phonograph complete with cylinder records. $720 £360

Fine diamond disc phonograph in Chippendale style cabinet, American, circa 1925. $960 £480

Bell 'Gem' phonograph complete with seventy-one wax cylinder records in their original boxes. $980 £490

Good and rare Edison spring motor phonograph in oak cabinet, American, circa 1896-1900. $1,460 £730

Edison Home phonograph with Bettini attachment. $2,340 £1,300

Rare tin foil phonograph, circa 1879. $4,600 £2,300

PIANOS

An upright piano by F. Rosener, Berlin, in an ebonised case. $70 £35

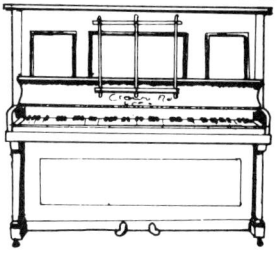

A mahogany upright piano by Gresham & Co., London, 4ft.9in. wide. $80 £40

Edwardian inlaid mahogany piano. $80 £40

An upright piano by Benson, in a fine mahogany case. $90 £45

An upright grand pianoforte by Vyner in a mahogany case. $100 £50

An ebonised upright piano by H. Lange & Co., Madgeburgh, the front panel extensively fretted, 4ft.9in. wide. $100 £50

PIANOS

An ebonised upright piano by James, 4ft.11in. wide. $110 £55

An upright pianoforte by John Brinsmead & Sons, London, in a walnut inlaid case. $110 £55

A fine upright piano by Challen, in walnut case. $120 £60

19th century upright iron framed pianoforte by Cramer & Co. of London. $130 £65

A semi-grand pianoforte by C. Goetze, in white painted case. $140 £70

Kaim and John upright grand pianoforte, six and a half octave, in rosewood inlaid case. $150 £75

PIANOS

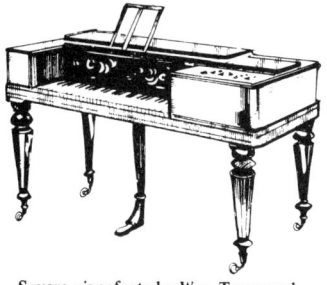

Square pianoforte by Wm. Townsend & Son, in a mahogany case, 5ft.10in. wide. $150 £75

An upright pianoforte by Lambert, London, in a rosewood case. $160 £80

Iron framed piano by Kirkman, London, in a walnut case. $160 £80

Grand piano by Broadwood in a rosewood case, 7ft. long. $160 £80

19th century walnut cased upright iron framed piano by King Brothers of London. $170 £85

Ship's piano by Cramer, in stained wood case. $180 £90

PIANOS

A semi-grand pianoforte by Bluthner, in ebonised case. $190 £95

An upright pianoforte by Chappell in mahogany case. $190 £95

A semi-grand piano by Collard & Collard in a rosewood case. $190 £95

A walnut grand piano by Ernst Kaps, Dresden, on octagonal tapering legs, 6ft. deep. $230 £115

Mid 19th century, mahogany framed, table piano, by Collard & Collard, London. $240 £120

An upright piano by Benson, in a mahogany case. $264 £132

PIANOS

Regency cross banded mahogany cased square piano with inlaid and open brass work to backboard, on screw-in fluted supports. $264 £132

A Victorian rosewood square pianoforte by Collard & Collard 6ft.4in. wide. $290 £145

Regency table piano by Muirwood & Co., Edinburgh, 167cm. wide. $320 £160

A rosewood semi-grand piano by John Broadwood & Sons, 6ft. long. $340 £170

An upright grand piano by Challen, in a fine mahogany case. $350 £175

A semi-grand pianoforte by Hagspiel and Co., Dresden in a burr walnut case. $350 £175

PIANOS

An early Victorian mahogany and ebony inlaid square pianoforte, on turned and fluted legs, by Wood, Small & Co. $370 £185

A rosewood boudoir grand piano by Collard & Collard, 5ft.3in. long. $430 £215

19th century baby grand piano by Hagspiel & Co. of Dresden, in an ebonised case. $440 £220

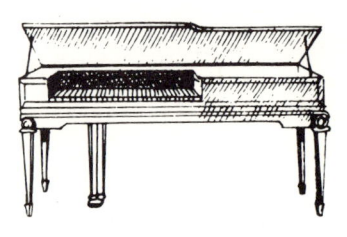

Early 19th century table piano in working order. $440 £220

A Steck pianola piano in mahogany case with a few rolls of music and a box seat piano stool. $540 £270

Early 19th century upright grand piano by Broadwood. $540 £270

PIANOS

A semi-grand pianoforte by Ed Seiler, Liegnitz, in a rosewood case.
$540 £270

An upright grand piano by C. Bechstein, in a mahogany case, No. 139370. $600 £300

Broadwood piano in mahogany case, 66in. long, circa 1840.
$640 £320

A Collard & Collard boudoir grand pianoforte in a mahogany case, 156cm. long. $470 £235

Monington & Weston baby grand pianoforte No. 56600, in a mahogany case, 5ft.3in. long.
$720 £360

Semi-grand pianoforte by Bluthner, Leipzig, in an ebonised case.
$720 £360

PIANOS

A baby grand pianoforte in mahogany case on square tapered legs, by Cooper Southam, London. $740 £370

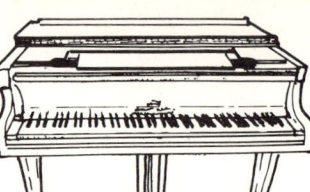

Marshall and Rose baby grand pianoforte in mahogany case, 4ft.6in. long. $770 £385

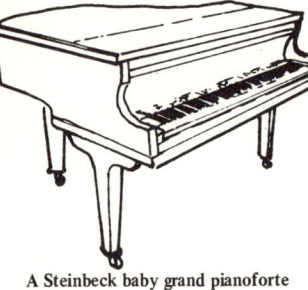

A Steinbeck baby grand pianoforte in a rosewood case, 122cm. long. $840 £420

A large and ornate upright piano by Steinway & Sons, New York, each surface with carved and gilt scrolls on a green ground, 5ft.4in. wide. $840 £420

A boudoir grand pianoforte, in rosewood case, on square tapered legs, by John Brinsmead & Sons, London. $840 £420

An ebonised boudoir grand piano by R. Goss & Kallmann, Berlin, (No. 59312), on square tapered legs. $860 £430

PIANOS

A most unusual and nicely decorated French piano, by Soufleto for the 1871 exhibition, 54in. wide, 49in. high, 26in. deep. $900 £450

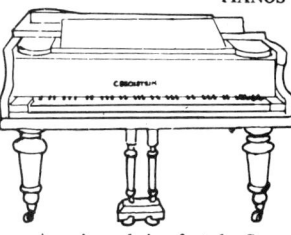

A semi-grand pianoforte by C. Bechstein in rosewood case, No. 106037. $960 £480

A rosewood inlaid, semi-grand piano by Steinway & Sons, Hamburg, 6ft. long. $960 £480

Grand pianoforte by Wm. Stodard & Son, London, circa 1830, 6ft.11in. long. $1,010 £505

Art Nouveau piano by Broadwood. $1,200 £600

Boudoir grand piano by Collard & Collard, rosewood case inlaid satinwood, 72in. long. $1,340 £670

PIANOS

A Bechstein (C) boudoir grand pianoforte in rosewood case, No. 61450, 6ft.9in. long.
$1,340 £670

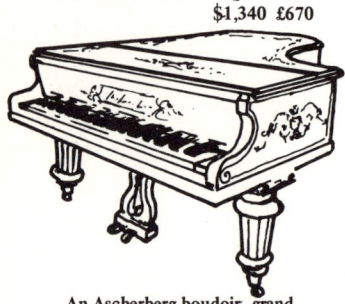

An Ascherberg boudoir grand pianoforte, seven octave, in a rosewood and marquetry case, 203cm. long. $1,440 £720

Square piano by Adam Beyer, London 1785, 4ft.9¼in. long.
$1,490 £745

Early 19th century portable piano by Joseph Klein, Vienna, 30in. long.
$1,440 £720

George III mahogany conductor's piano, striking on glass bars, 23in. wide, 23in. deep, 33½in. high. $1,440 £720

19th century Broadwood japanned boudoir grand piano. $1,500 £750

PIANOS

French combined piano and toilet table, circa 1820, 28in. long. $1,520 £760

Square piano by Longman & Broderip, London, circa 1795, 5ft.2in. long. $1,560 £780

19th century upright overstrung iron frame piano by Monington and Weston in a boulle and ormolu decorated case. $1,800 £900

Mid 19th century Viennese Giraffe piano, 7ft.7in. high, in rosewood case. $1,870 £935

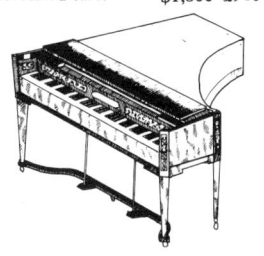

Viennese grand pianoforte by Anton Walter & Son, circa 1815, 5ft.11in. long. $1,920 £960

A very fine French red boulle and ebony upright piano, by L. Benoite, Paris, with chased brass borders, mounts, candlesticks and side handles, 4ft.8in. wide. $2,040 £1,020

PIANOS

A superb rosewood boudoir grand piano by Ascherberg of Dresden.
$2,160 £1,080

Unusual upright piano by Anton Màrtin Thym, Vienna, circa 1820, 5ft.6¼in. high. $2,160 £1,080

Square piano by John Broadwood, London 1792, 5ft.2½in. long. $2,260 £1,130

Sycamore cased baby grand by Strohmenger. $2,700 £1,350

A square piano by Chistopher Ganer, London 1784, 5ft. wide. $2,800 £1,400

Boudoir grand piano by John Broadwood, in a satinwood inlaid mahogany case. $3,080 £1,540

PIANOS

A square piano by Adam Beyer, London, 1773 4ft. 8¾in. wide. $3,100 £1,550

A square piano by Johannes Zumpe and Gabriel Buntebart, London 1770. $3,300 £1,650

Grand pianoforte by John Broadwood & Sons, London, circa 1815, 8ft.1½in. long. $3,520 £1,760

An exceptionally fine piano by Garrati of Rome, circa 1880, with eleven painted panels and heavily decorated with ormolu. $3,850 £1,925

English grande piano-forte by John Broadwood and Son, London 1804, 7ft. 5½in. long. $4,000 £2,000

French Giraffe piano, circa 1830, 7ft. 6in. high. $4,400 £2,200

PIANOS

French cased piano by John Broadwood, circa 1870. $4,620 £2,310

Louis XV style tulipwood salon piano inset with superb porcelain plaques and having fine ormolu embellishments. $5,720 £2,860

Late 18th century grand piano by Broadwood. $5,940 £2,970

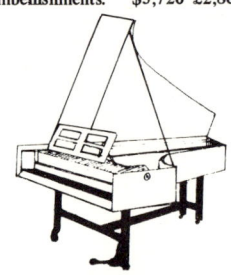

A pianoforte by Clementi, circa 1800. $6,050 £3,025

19th century kingwood and marquetry grand piano with ormolu mounts by Erard of Paris. $5,580 £3,100

An exceptionally fine late 19th century Erard grand piano profusely decorated with ormolu. $13,200 £6,600

PIANINO

Pianino by Chappel and Co., mahogany case inlaid with ebony stringing, 22½in. wide, circa 1830. $600 £300

PICCOLO

Simple system ebony piccolo with alternative flageolet mouthpiece, 11½in. long. $70 £35

POCHETTE

Late 18th century French pochette, total length 17½in. $960 £480

Mid 18th century German pochette, 19¼in. long. $1,870 £935

POLYPHONES

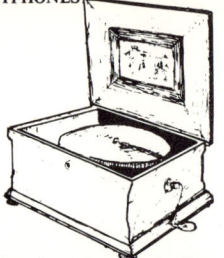

Victorian walnut cased table polyphone with eight 15in. metal discs, the lid inset with a little sepia print of cherubs. $340 £170

Victorian polyphone with eight 10in. discs. $380 £190

Table polyphone by Adler. $620 £310

German, late 19th century polyphone with seven metal discs, 1ft.9in. wide. $620 £310

Mahogany cased miniature polyphone, complete with twelve discs. $640 £320

Victorian walnut cased polyphone. $720 £360

POLYPHONES

Late 19th century Stella polyphone in an inlaid case, 29in. wide, with seven discs. $770 £385

Victorian 'Penny in the Slot' polyphone. $960 £480

A fine German mahogany cabinet polyphone on stand with twenty discs, 2ft.2in. wide, 6ft.4in. high. $1,250 £625

Stella table polyphone with twenty-two metal discs. $1,800 £900

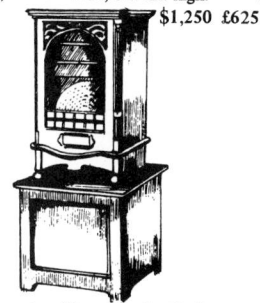

19th century 'Penny in the Slot' polyphone with forty-six discs, each 19½in. diameter. $1,680 £840

19th century 'Penny in the Slot' polyphone. $2,000 £1,000

RADIOS

Gecophone (BBC) in mahogany case. $40 £20

English celestion radio speaker in mahogany cabinet. $44 £22

An English amplion radio speaker in domed wooden case. $68 £34

A radiogram in mahogany serpentine fronted cabinet. $80 £40

RECORDERS

Mid 18th century English flute or recorder. 24ins. long. $1,560 £780

An important 18th century treble recorder by T. Stanesby, Jnr., London, 19¾in. long. $5,000 £2,500

Rare and important late 17th century treble recorder by Joseph Bradbury, 30½in. long. $6,400 £3,200

REGAL

Mid 18th century French Regal in walnut case, 38½in. long. $2,640 £1,320

SACKBUT

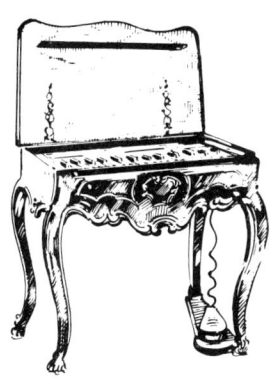

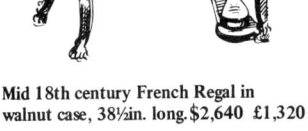

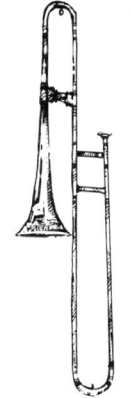

Rare Swiss Sackbut by Jacob Steimer, Zofingen, early 18th century, length of tube without mouthpiece 105½in.
$6,160 £3,080

SALTERIO TEDESCO

Rare Salterio Tedesco by Gion Zino, Brescia 1692, maximum length 3ft.11in.
$1,200 £600

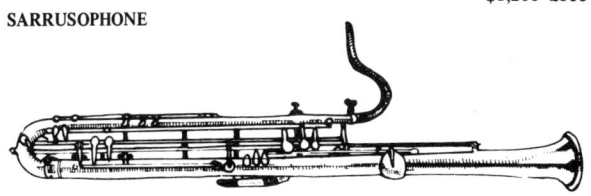

SARRUSOPHONE

Tenor sarrusophone, mid 19th century, 28in. long. $500 £250

SERPENTS

An English serpent, possibly by Thomas Key of London, circa 1810. $900 £450

Five keyed serpent by B. Huggett, circa 1835, 74cm. high. $980 £490

SITAR

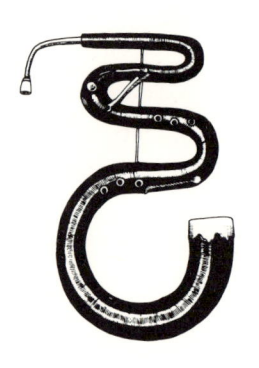

English serpent by D'Almaine & Co., London, early 19th century, length 7ft.7in. $1,100 £550

A small early 19th century sitar. $130 £65

SPINETS

George III spinet by John Broadwood of London with four octaves.
$1,200 £600

Mid 18th century mahogany cased spinet by Joseph Harris of London.
$1,680 £840

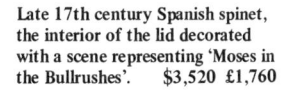

Late 17th century Spanish spinet, the interior of the lid decorated with a scene representing 'Moses in the Bullrushes'. $3,520 £1,760

English spinet by John Harrison, London, 1781, 73½in. wide.
$5,000 £2,500

SPINETS

Important spinet by Joseph Tisserant and Benjamin Slade, London, circa 1700, 65in. long. $6,120 £3,400

Important spinet by Muchel Richard, Paris, 1690, 26½in. long keyboard. $14,550 £7,500

SYMPHONION ACCORDION

Symphonion by Charles Wheatstone, London, circa 1830, 2¾in. high. $960 £480

Rare Charles Wheatstone symphonion accordion with four parallel rows of ivory finger studs, 2in. high, circa 1829. $1,490 £745

SYMPHONION

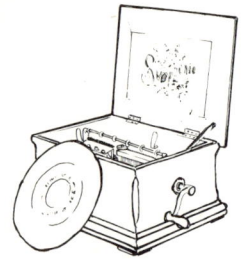

Late 19th century German 10½in. symphonion disc musical box, 1ft.6in. wide, sold with nine metal discs. $820 £410

German walnut marquetry symphonion on stand and forty-seven discs, circa 1880, 1ft.10in. wide, 2ft.10in. high. $860 £430

SYMPHONION

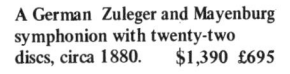

A German Zuleger and Mayenburg symphonion with twenty-two discs, circa 1880. $1,390 £695

Late 19th century German 19.1/8in wall hanging symphonion disc musical box, 4ft.5in. high, with ten discs. $2,860 £1,430

TIBETAN HORNS

A copper and brass Tibetan horn. $50 £25

A Tibetan copper and brass horn. $60 £30

Tibetan copper and brass horn with chased plate mounts, 5ft.8in. $130 £65

TRUMPETS

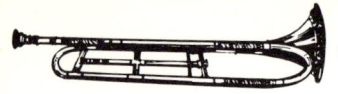

A good quality herald's silver-plated trumpet with slide valve, by H. Potter of London. $90 £45

A herald's silver-plated trumpet by H. Potter of London. $100 £50

Tibetan trumpet made from a human thigh bone. $110 £55

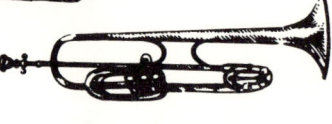

A good quality herald's silver-plated trumpet, by H. Potter, London. $110 £55

Unusual trumpet by Kohler, London, 24in. long, circa 1865. $243 £135

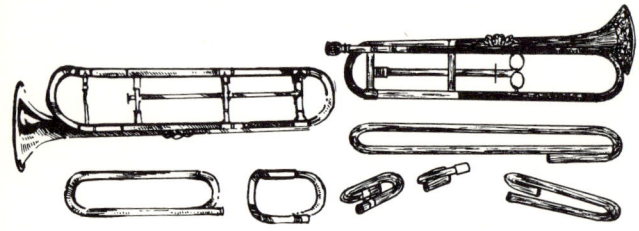

Brass slide trumpet by Hawkes and Son, London, with two tuning crooks. $310 £155

Slide trumpet by James Goodison of London, 22¾in. long, in the original rosewood veneered box. $1,200 £600

VIOLS

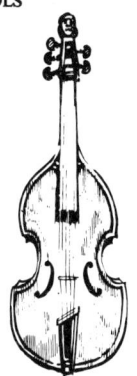

Mid 18th century French pardessus de viole, unlabelled, length of back 12½in. $2,160 £1,080

Italian tenor viol de gamba by Giovanni Pietro Guarneri, Mantua, 1689, body 18in. $6,930 £3,465

Rare tenor viol, mid 18th century, by Frederick Hintz, London, length of back 17½in. $8,000 £4,000

VIOLAS

An old viola after Stradivarius with bow and case. $100 £50

American viola by W.H. Patten, New Hampshire, 1909, with two bows, length of back 16¼in. $1,010 £505

French viola by Apparut & Hilaire, Mirecourt, 1971, length of back 16in. $1,300 £650

VIOLAS

Fine viola by Charles J.B. Collin-Mezin, Paris, 1949, length of back 16in. $1,320 £660

French viola by Leon Bernardel, Paris 1914, length of back 16in. $1,320 £660

An Italian viola attributed to E. Ceruti, Cremona, 1847. $1,560 £780

Fine viola by William H. Luff, London 1969, length of back 15¾in. $1,800 £900

Viola by Percy Lee, London 1912, length of back 16¼in, in shaped case. $1,800 £900

A viola by Johann Blasius Weigert, Linz, 1724, length of back 16¼in. $2,040 £1,020

VIOLAS

Viola D'Amore by Michael Ignatius Stadlmann, 1792, length of back 15in.
$2,400 £1,200

Viola by Mathias Albani, Busani, 1690, length of back 15¾in.
$2,800 £1,400

Viola by Richard Duke, London 1768, length of back 16½in, in shaped case.
$2,750 £1,375

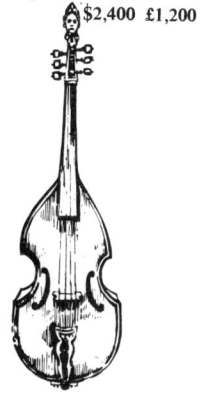

Interesting viola bastarda, unlabelled, length of back 25¾in.
$3,410 £1,705

Viola by Georges Adolfe Chanit, Manchester, 1895, length of back 16¼in, with silver mounted bow.
$3,520 £1,760

Interesting viola labelled Gio. Paolo Magini in Brescia, length of back 15¾in.
$3,850 £1,925

VIOLAS

Fine English viola by Samuel Gilkes, London 1819, length of back 15½in. $3,960 £1,980

Fine Italian viola by Tomaso Eberle, Naples 1777, length of back 15½in. $6,600 £3,300

17th century viola of the Brescian School. $9,900 £4,950

A superb 19th century viola by Jean Baptiste Vuillaume, circa 1872. $10,000 £5,000

Viola by Joannes Franciscus Pressenda, Turin 1826, length of back 15½in. $17,000 £8,500

Viola by Joannes Franciscus Pressenda, 1826. $18,000 £9,000

VIOLINS (MUTE)   VIOLINS

Composite English mute violin with oval sound box, length of back 14¼in. $340 £170

Unusual English mute violin, 1874, length of body 14in. $530 £265

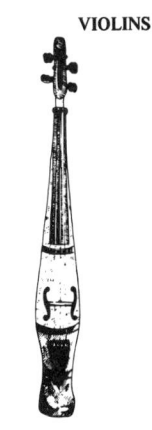

Early 19th century mute violin, total length 24½in. $960 £480

VIOLINS

A satinwood and pine violin and a bow in a wooden case. $30 £15

An Edwardian youth's violin and bow, in a case. $40 £20

A violin with bow in fitted wooden case, 1ft.7in. long. $44 £22

VIOLINS

A violin with pine and satinwood case, labelled Chas. Adin, 1888, Manchester. $44 £22

An Italian violin with pine and satinwood case, labelled 'Maggini', Dentiche Arbuit, 2ft. long. $50 £25

A Scottish violin, with pine and satinwood case, labelled George Duncan, Glasgow, 1889, and two bows. $110 £55

Bavarian violin, length of back 14in., in case. $108 £60

German violin, Bavarian school, length of back, 14in., circa 1820. $126 £70

Unlabelled English violin, length of back, 13¼in. $216 £120

VIOLINS

French violin by
C.A. Miremont,
Paris 1873,
length of back
14in. $480 £240

English violin, length
of back 14in.
$468 £260

An English violin
by N. Cross,
London, circa
1730-40, back
14in. long. $620 £310

American violin
circa 1900,
length of back
14in. $660 £330

Norwegian Hardanger-
felen, 1897, length of
back 14¼in.
$648 £360

English violin, length
of back, 14¼in., sold
with two bows.
$666 £370

VIOLINS

Violin by Sebastian Kloz, 1745, length of back 14in. $756 £420

Miniature violin by J. Wischer, Winterthour, 1852, length of back 4¾in. $790 £395

A Scandinavian Hardanger fiddle, dated 1877. $912 £456

Mid 18th century Mittenwald violin, sold with bow, length of back 14in. $940 £470

Late 19th century rectangular French violin by Jules Grandjon, Paris, length of back 14½in. $1,010 £505

Fine violin by Andrea Guarneri, Cremona, circa 1680, length of back 14in. $1,010 £505

VIOLINS

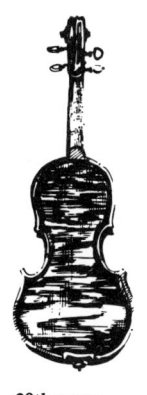

20th century Italian violin, length of back 14in. $1,150 £575

18th century French violin, length of back 14ins. $1,150 £575

Italian violin by Guiseppe Rossi, Rome 1914, length of back 14in. $1,200 £600

A fine violin by John Furber, made in 1801 and bearing the maker's manuscript label. $1,200 £600

Fine French violin by Jerome Thibouville-Lamy, length of back 14in, with silver mounted bow. $1,250 £625

Violin with monogram A.S. length of back 14½in, and one silver mounted bow. $1,250 £625

VIOLINS

A violin by Paul Bailly, Paris 1890, back 14in. long. $1,250 £625

English violin by Henry Jay, London 1776, length of back 14in. $1,300 £650

Violin by Arthur Richardson, Crediton, Devon, 1921, length of back 14in. $1,320 £660

Interesting Flemish violin, probably by Mathias Hofmans, Antwerp, circa 1680, length of back 14in. $1,390 £695

Early 20th century Italian violin by Vicenzo Sannino, Naples, length of back 14in. $1,440 £720

French violin by Amedee Dominique Dieudonne, Mirecourt 1946, length of back 14in. $1,440 £720

VIOLINS

A violin by A.G. Bergamer, back 14¼in. long. $1,440 £720

Violin by George Craske, length of back 14¼in. $1,440 £720

Unlabelled German violin, Nurenberg School, length of back 14in, in shaped wooden case. $1,560 £780

French violin by Honore Derazey, Mirecourt, circa 1860, in shaped case, length of back 14¼in. $1,630 £815

An Italian violin by A. Lorenzi, 1793, back 14¼in. long. $1,680 £840

French violin by Marc Laberte, 1955, length of back 14in. $1,800 £900

VIOLINS

19th century carved violin, Dutch or German, length of back 14in. $1,800 £900

Mittenwald violin by Mathias Hornsteiner, 1781, length of back 14in. $1,860 £930

French violin by Paul Bailly, Paris 1884, signed in ink, length of back 14in. $1,920 £960

An Italian violin labelled Santino Lavazza, circa 1800, 14in. long. $2,040 £1,020

Interesting violin, probably Italian, length of back 14in, sold with silver mounted bow. $2,040 £1,020

Fine violin by Paul Bailly, signed, length of back 14in, in shaped case. $2,040 £1,020

VIOLINS

Violin by George Kloz, 1753, length of back 14¼in. $2,160 £1,080

Italian violin, labelled Giovanni Grancino Contrada di Milan 1693, length of back 14in, circa 1840, with a silver mounted bow. $2,160 £1,080

French violin by Charles J.B. Collin-Mezin, Paris 1896, length of back 14¼in, in shaped case. $2,160 £1,080

Italian violin by Aristide Cavalli, Cremona 1923, length of back 14in. $2,160 £1,080

French violin by Jean Francois Aldric, Paris 1798, length of back 14in, and one ivory mounted violin bow. $2,280 £1,140

Violin by Jacob Stainer Absam 1665, length of back 14in, in leather case. $2,280 £1,140

VIOLINS

A Mittenwald violin by Aegidius Klotz, 1764. $2,400 £1,200

Italian violin by Aloysi Soffriti 1892, length of back 14in. $2,400 £1,200

A fine violin by Giulio Degani, Venice 1902, length of back 14.1/8in. $2,400 £1,200

A fine unlabelled French violin, circa 1840, back 14in. long. $2,420 £1,210

Violin by Pietro Dosi, Bologna, 1860, labelled, length of back 14in. $2,420 £1,210

Italian violin by Ferdinando Alberti, Milan, circa 1740, length of back 14in. $2,600 £1,300

VIOLINS

An Italian violin by G. Scarampella Varese, 1902, back 14½in. long. $2,600 £1,300

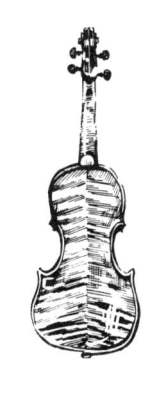

Tyrolese violin, 1710, length of back 14in, with silver mounted bow. $2,600 £1,300

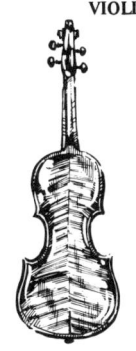

Fine violin by Matthius Kloz, Mittenwald, late 17th century, length of back 14in. $2,640 £1,320

Mid 19th century French violin, with a silver mounted bow, length of back 14in. $2,640 £1,320

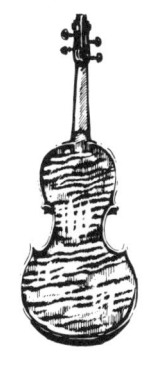

Italian violin by Gartono Pollastri Bologna 1951, length of back 14in. $2,640 £1,320

Fine violin by Aegidius Kloz, Mittenwald, 1729, length of back 14¼in. $2,640 £1,320

VIOLINS

A violin by G. Pollastri, Bologna 1932, length of back 14in.
$2,750 £1,375

A French violin labelled J.B. Vuillaume, length of back 14½in.
$2,860 £1,430

Italian violin by Vincanzo Postiglione, Naples 1913, length of back 14in.
$3,300 £1,650

Miniature violin by John Shaw, Manchester 1905.
$3,520 £1,760

Mid 17th century violin by Jacob Stainer, Absam, length of back 14in. $3,630 £1,815

Attractive miniature violin by John Shaw, Manchester 1905, length of back 2¾in.
$3,520 £1,760

VIOLINS

Italian violin by Gioffredo Cappa, Saluzzo, late 17th century, length of back 14in.
$3,850 £1,925

Important Italian violin by Petrus Guarnerius of Mantua, 1702, length of back 14in. $3,960 £1,980

Italian violin by Joannes Francesco Pressenda, Turin 1840, length of back 14in.
$4,180 £2,090

Important violin by Joannes Baptista Guadagnini, Parma 1761, length of back 13¾in, in a fitted case by W.E. Hill & Sons. $4,400 £2,200

Fine violin by Dario D'Attili, New York, 1963, length of back 14in. $4,620 £2,310

Violin by Jacob Fendt, London, unlabelled, length of back 14in.
$5,280 £2,640

VIOLINS

Italian violin labelled Giovanni Paulo Magini, Brescia 1615, length of back 14¼in.
$5,500 £2,750

Italian violin by Joannes Gagliano, Naples 1803, length of back 14in. $5,720 £2,860

A violin probably by a later member of the Gaudagnini family, 1756.
$5,720 £2,860

Fine violin by Joannes Francesco Pressenda, 1852, length of back 14in, in shaped case.
$6,050 £3,025

Violin by Thomas Balestri, Mantua 1760, length of back 15in. $6,600 £3,300

Violin by Joseph and Antonius Gagliano, Naples, about 1790.
$7,040 £3,520

VIOLINS

Italian violin by
Giovanni Paulo
Magini, Brescia,
length of back
14½in. long.
$7,260 £3,630

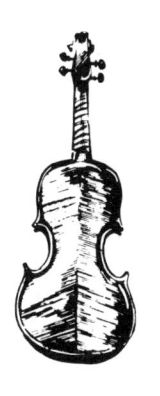

Fine Italian violin by
Giovanni Battista
Zanoli, Verona, circa
1780, length of back
14in. $7,480 £3,740

Violin by Guiseppe
Guadagnini, Parma,
late 18th century,
length of back
14½in. $7,480 £3,740

Fine violin by
Hannibal Fagnola
of Turin, circa
1890, length of
back 14in.
$7,920 £3,960

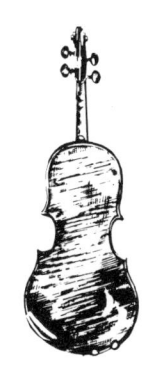

A violin by Joseph
Rocca, Turin 1844,
length of back 14in.
$7,920 £3,960

Violin by Antonius
and Hieronymus
Amati, Cremona
1625, length of
back 14in.
$8,800 £4,400

113

VIOLINS

Italian violin by Alexander Gagliano, Naples 1710, length of back 13¼in, in a leather case. $9,240 £4,620

Violin by T. Eberle, Naples. $9,240 £4,620

Late 18th century Italian violin by Pietro Giovanni Mantegazza, Milan, length of back 13½in. $9,680 £4,840

Italian violin by Alexander Gagliano, Naples 1724, length of back 13½in, gold mounted rosewood pegs. $10,560 £5,280

Italian violin by Carlo Ferdinando Landolfi, Milan 1766, length of back 14in. $10,560 £5,280

Italian violin by Giovanni Battista Gabrielli, Florence, circa 1760, length of back, 14in. $11,220 £5,610

VIOLINS

Italian violin by Joseph Gagliano, Naples 1769, length of back 14in, in leather case. $12,000 £6,000

Italian violin by Bartholomeo Tassini, Venice, circa 1750, length of back 14in. $13,200 £6,600

Italian violin by Giovanni Battista Gabrielli, Florence, circa 1760, length of back 14in. $14,080 £7,040

Violin by Antonio Stradivari, Cremona, in the Amateur style, circa 1670-75, 14in. long. $14,300 £7,150

Italian violin by Andrea Guarneri, Cremona 1663, length of back 14in. $16,280 £8,140

Violin by Joseph Gagliano, Naples, 1780, length of back 14in. $16,720 £8,360

VIOLINS

Italian violin by Antonius and Hieronymus Amati, Cremona, 1618, length of back, 14in. $17,160 £8,580

Italian violin by Joseph Gagliano, Naples 1782, length of back 14in, with bow. $18,700 £9,350

Violin by Joseph Rocca, Turin, 1856, length of back 14in, with silver mounted bow. $21,560 £10,780

Italian violin by Tommaso Balestrieri, Mantua, length of back 14in, in shaped leather case. $23,000 £11,500

Important violin by Francesco Ruggeri, Cremona 1691, length of back 14in, with a silver mounted violin bow. $26,000 £13,000

Violin by Pietro Dosi, Bologna 1860, labelled, length of back 14in. $30,000 £15,000

VIOLINS

'The Loder' by
Antonio Stradivari.
$33,000 £16,500

Violin by Omobono
Stradivari, Cremona
1714, length of
back 14in. $34,000 £17,000

A violin by G.
Guarneri,
Cremona 1707.
$37,000 £18,500

Important violin by
Antonio Stradivari,
Cremona 1697,
length of back 14in.
$76,000 £38,000

The 'Mackenzie
Stradivari' violin,
Cremona 1685,
length of back
14in. $100,000 £50,000

The Lady Blunt
violin by
Stradivari.
$170,000 £85,000

VIOLIN CASES

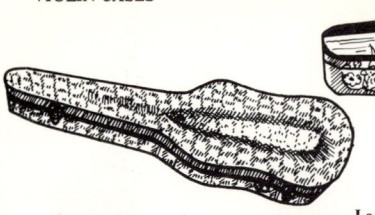

Leather covered violin case with velvet interior. $40 £20

Lacquered violin case extensively inlaid with mother-of-pearl in a peacock design. $300 £150

Mid 19th century North Italian violin case with fruitwood marquetry inlay, 31¼in. long. $550 £275

A good violin case bound in tooled and gilded green roan leather. $1,060 £530

Unusual Japanese Lac Burgate violin case, 31½in. long. $1,220 £610

Fine satinwood violin case by W.E. Hill & Sons, London, 30½in. long. $2,160 £1,080

VIOLONCELLOS

An interesting unlabelled violoncello, length of back 29½in. $960 £480

A Violoncello piccolo bearing a manuscript label J. Steiner 1669, back 23in. long. $1,490 £745

Interesting violoncello unlabelled, circa 1780, length of back 30in. $1,560 £780

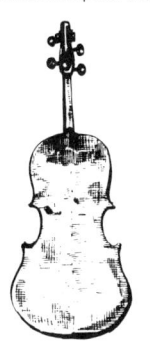

An English violoncello by T. Kennedy School, back 29in. long. $1,870 £935

Interesting violoncello labelled Fato in Gerona di Giacamo Zanoni 1751, length of back 29in. $2,160 £1,080

Milanese violoncello labelled 'Paulo Antonion Testori Milano Ao 1745', length of back 13¼in. $2,640 £1,320

VIOLONCELLOS

Violoncello by William Forster, London, circa 1820, length of back 29¾in. $2,640 £1,320

English violoncello, probably by Thomas Kennedy, London, circa 1810, length of back 28¾in. $3,740 £1,870

Fine violoncello by Thomas Kennedy, London 1819, length of back 29in. $4,400 £2,200

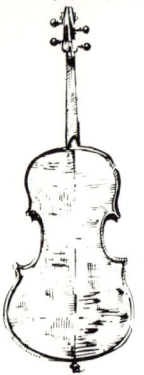

Violoncello by Antonius and Hieronymus Amati, Cremona, 1559, length of back 28¾in. $5,280 £2,640

A violoncello by Guiseppe Pedrazzini, Milano, 1922. $5,720 £2,860

Violoncello by Henrick Jacobs, Amsterdam 1676, length of back 21in. $6,600 £3,300

VIOLONCELLOS

Very fine violoncello by William Forster, London 1791, length of back 29in. $7,480 £3,740

Violoncello by Joseph Panormo, London, unlabelled, length of back 29¾in. $8,360 £4,180

An unlabelled violoncello with varnish of golden brown, back 19½in. long. $13,640 £6,820

Important violoncello by Jean Baptiste Vuillaume, Paris, length of back 29¾in. $20,900 £10,450

French violoncello by Jean Baptiste Vuillaume, circa 1840, length of back 29½in. $21,120 £10,560

Italian violoncello by Carlo Antonio Testore, Milan 1725, length of back 30in. $22,000 £11,000

VIRGINALS

Late 17th century Italian virginals in a leather bound case, 8in. long. $1,080 £540

Late 19th century Italian virginals, 21¼in. wide. $1,740 £870

Italian polygonal virginals attributed to Pasquinus Quericus, Florence, 1610, 5ft.5¼in. long. $5,280 £2,640

Highly important double virginals by Hans Ruckers the Younger, Antwerp 1623, 5ft.7¼in. long. $84,000 £42,000

ZITHERS

A Victorian zither. $60 £30

Late 19th century zither complete with case. $100 £50

Fine quality 19th century zither. $130 £65

INDEX

Abrahams, B.H. 53
Absam, Jacob 107
Accordion 10
Adin, Chas. 101
Adler 86
Albani, Mathias 97
Alberti, Ferdinando 108
Aldric, J.F. 107
Alexandra 50
Amati, A. 113, 116, 120
American Fiddle 10
Apollo Gramophone 34
Apparut & Hilaire 95
A.S. 103
Ascherberg 80, 81
Astor, George 61
Atton, Michele 21
Autoharp 50
Automaton Figures 8, 9

Bagpipes 10
Bailly, Paul 104, 106
Bainbridge, W.M. 27
Balestri, Thomas 112, 116
Banjos 11
Barrel Organs 12, 13
Bates, A.C.T. 12
Battente Chitarra 38
Bechstein, C. 77, 79, 80
Bells In Sight 53-55, 58
Beltona 30
Benoite, L. 81
Benson 71, 74
Bergamer, A.G. 105

Berliner Gramophone 35
Bernardel, Leon 96
Beyer, Adam 80, 83
Bible Organ 63
Blackman 28
Bluthner 74, 77
Bolton, Richard John 22
Boosey & Co. 21
Bows 14-18
Bradbury, Joseph 88
Bremond 58
Bremond & Greiner 57
Brinsmead, John 72, 78
Broadcaster, The 11
Broadwood 73, 75-77, 79, 80, 82, 83, 91
Buffet 22
Bugles 19
Buntebart, Gabriel 83

Cahusac, T. 61
Cahusac, Thomas 28
Cappa, Gioffredo 111
Car Horn 51
Caron 46
Cat Tea Party 8
Cavalli, Aristide 107
Cecilium 20
Cello 20
Ceruti, E. 96
Ceterone 20
Challen 72, 75
Chamber Organ 64
Chanit, G.A. 97

Chappell 74, 85
Chitarra Battente 38
Chitarrone 21
Clarinets 22
Clavichords 22
Clementi 83
Clementi & Co. 19, 27, 28
Coaching Horns 44
Cobby, J.C. 46
Coca Cola 50
Cocks, R. 49
Collard & Collard 74-77, 79
Collin-Mezin, C.J.B. 96, 107
Columbia 31, 35, 36, 65, 67
Competition Organ 63
Concertina 50
Conductor's Piano 80
Contrada, Giovanni 107
Cooper Southam 78
Cor Anglais 23
Cor De Chasse 44
Cornets 21
Cornopeans 24
Couenophone 24
Courtois, Antoine 21
Cousineau 41
Cramer & Co. 72, 73
Crampion & Co. 22
Craske, George 105
Cross, Nathaniel 99, 101
Cymbalist Automaton 9

D'Almaine & Co. 22, 90
D'Attili, Dario 111

Debain, A.F. 39
Degani, Giulio 108
Derazey, Honore 105
Dieudonne, Amedee D. 104
Disc Organette 63
Dodd, John 14, 16, 17
Dosi, Pietro 108, 116
Drouet, Louis 28, 29
Drums 25, 26
Duke, Richard 97
Duncan 101
Duophone 35

East India Co. 25
Eberle, Tomaso 98, 114
Eblin, Thomas 26
Edison Bell 32, 65, 70
Edison Gem 65
Egan, J. 40
E.M.G. 41
Erard 39-41, 83, 84
Esrar 27
Euphonium 27
Eury 15
Evv Matheus 37

Fabrica, Stridente 48
Fabricatore Gennard 37
Fagnola, Hannibal 113
Fendt, Jacob 111
Fetique, Victor 16
Finkel, J.S. 15
Flageolets 27
Flutes 28, 29
Forster, William 120, 121

Gabrielli, G.B. 114, 115
Gagliano, Alexander 114
Gagliano, Antonius 112
Gagliano, Johannes 112
Gagliano, Joseph 115, 116
Ganer, Christopher 82
Gantley, Lord 18
Garrati 82
Gavioli 12

G.C. & Co. 66, 68
Gecophone 88
Gilkes, Samuel 98
Ginn, E.M. 30
Giraffe Piano 81, 83
Goetze, C. 72
Goff, Thomas 46
Golding & Co. 22
Goodison, James 94
Gordon Tartan 10
Goss & Kallmann 78
Gramophones 30-35
Gramophone & Typewriter Ltd. 33
Grandjon, Jules 102
Graphophones 36
Gresham & Co. 71
Guadagnini, Guiseppe 113
Guadagnini, J.B. 111, 112
Guarneri, Andrea 102, 115
Guarneri, G. 117
Guarneri, Giovanni P. 95
Guarnerius, Petrus 111
Guitars 36, 37, 38

Haas Family 45
Hadaway, Robert 20
Hagspiel & Co. 75, 76
Hampshire Regiment 25
Hans The Younger 43
Hardanger Fiddle 102
Harley 47
Harmonicor 38
Harmonium 39
Harps 39-41
Harpsichords 42, 43
Harris & Nixon 45
Harris, Joseph. 91
Harrison, John 91
Hawkes & Co. 94
Hill, Henry 28, 29
Hill, W.E. 14-18, 111, 118
H.M.V. 31
Hintz, Frederick 95
Hofmans, Mathias 104
Hofmaster, John C. 44

Hook Harp 40
Horne, Robert 25
Horns 44-45
Hornsteiner, Mathias 106
Huggett, B. 90
Hunting Horns 45, 46
Hurdy Gurdies 46

Imhof & Mukle 64

Jacobs, Henryck 120
James 72
Jaulin, Louis Jules 38
Jay, Henry 47, 104
Jumeau, E. 8, 9

Kaim & John 72
Kallippe 53
Kammerer & Reinhardt 35
Kaps, Ernst 74
Kennedy, T. 119, 120
Key, Thomas 24, 90
King Bros. 5
Kirckman 73
Kirckman, Abraham 42
Kirckman, Jacob 42, 43
Kits 46
Klein, Joseph 80
Klenig 61
Klotz, Aegidius 108, 109
Kloz, George 107
Kloz, Mathius 109
Knoeloch, Robert F. 57
Kohler, H. 24
Kusder, Henry 22

Laberte, Marc 105
Lafleur, Jacques 17
Lambert 73
Lambertphone 68
Landorff 60
Lange & Co. 71
Lavazza, Santino 106
Lee, Percy 96
Light, Edward 40

124

Longman & Broderip 81
Lorenzi, A. 105
Luff, William H. 96
Lumiere Gramophone 33
Lutes 46
Lyres 47
Lyrophonwerke 67

Maccaferri, Mario 37
Maggini 101
Magini, Gio P. 97, 112, 113
Maire, Nicolas 15
Mandolins 48
Mandoras 47
Mantegazza, Pietro 114
Maori Flute 29
Marshall & Rose 78
Mechanical Organ 64
Meissen 61
Mermond Freres 59
Metronomes 50-51
Millhouse, William 28
Miremont, C.A. 101
Mittenwald 102, 106
Mojon Manger & Co. 58
Monarch Gramophone 33
Monington & W. 77, 81
Monzani 27
Mougenot, Georges 17
Muirwood & Co. 75
Music Stands 49
Musical Boxes 52-60
Musician Automaton 8, 9
Mute Violins 100

Native Instrument 50
Nicole 54, 56, 57, 59, 60
Nigerian Oboe 61
Nipper 51
Norman, Barak 99
N.S.D.A.P. 19

Oboes 61
Ocarina 61
Octavino 62
Operaphone 62

Ophicleides 62
Orchestrion 64
Organs 63, 64
Orphica 62
Ott, Andreas 38
Ouchard, Emile F. 15, 16

Pace, F. 24
Padbury 51
Pageot, Simon 17
Paillard 57, 68
Panomo, George 20
Panormo, Joseph 121
Panormo, Louis 36
Parlophone 35
Pathe Horn 33, 34
Pathe Portable 31
Patten, W.H. 95
Pedrazzini, Guiseppe 120
Phipps & Robinson 45
Phonograph Doll 9
Phonographs 65-70
Pianino 85
Pianist Automaton 9
Pianola 76
Pianos 71-83
Piccolo 85
Pipe Organ 63
Pixie Grippa 30
Pochettes 85
Pollastri, Gartono 109, 110
Polyphones 85-87
Positive Organ 64
Potter, H. 94
Pressenda, Joannes F. 98, 111, 112
Preston, John 36, 37
Prior, William 36
Proser 29
Prowse, K. 59
Prowse, Keith 32

Quentin, Arthur 20
Quericus, Pasquinus 122

Radiogram 88
Radios 88

Rauche, Michael 36
Recorders 88
Regal 89
Reinhold & Co. 67
Remy, Jules 20
Renault 39
Richardson, Arthur 104
Robertson, James 10
Rocca, Joseph 113, 116
Rose Pompadour 54
Rosener, F. 71
Rossi, Guiseppe 103
Royal Scots 26
Ruckers, Hans 122
Rudall & Rose 28
Ruggeri, Francesco 116

Sackbut 89
Salterio Tedesco 89
Sannino, Vicenzo 104
Sarrusophone 89
Sartory, Eugene 15-18
Schmahl, George F. 23
Sciale, Guiseppe 36
Seiler, Ed. 77
Serpents 90
Shaman 26
Shaw, John 110
Sitar 90
Soffriti, Aloysi 108
Soufleto 79
Spinets 91, 92
Stadlmann, Michael I. 97
Stainer, Jacob 110
Stanesby, Thomas 29, 88
Stanesby, Thomas, Snr. 61
Steck 76
Steimer, Jacob 89
Steinbeck 78
Steiner, J. 119
Steinway & Sons 79
Stella Disc 58, 60
Stella Polyphone 85, 87
Stodard, Wm. 79
Stradivari, A. 115, 117
Stradivari, Antonio 47, 117

Stradivari, Omobono 117
Stradivarius 95
Strident 48
Svard, Sebastian 40
Symphonion 92, 93

Talbott, Sylvanus J. 10
Tassini, Bartholemeo 115
Taylor, Malcolm M. 14
Testore, Carlo A. 121
Testori, P.A. 119
Thai Drums 26
Thibouville-Lamy, J. 103
Thym, Martin 82
Tibetan Horns 93
Tibetan Oboe 61
Tielke, Joachim 46
Tourte, Francois 17
Townsend, Wm. 73
Triebert 21
Trumpets 94
Trute, Charles 43

Tubbs, James 15, 16, 18
Tull, Henry 42
Tuning Forks 51
Tyrolese Violin 109

Varese, G. Scarampella 109
Vaucher 57
Vaudry, Antoine 43
Viceroy, The 10
Vichy, G. 9
Vidoudez, Pierre 16
Vieira, Joao 48
Vinaccia 48
Viols 95
Violas 95-99
Violins 100-117
Violin Cases 118
Violoncellos 119-121
Virginals 122
Vuillaume, Jean B. 98, 110, 121
Vyner 71

Walter, Anton 81
Waterloo 18
Weidberg 43
Weidhaas, Paul 14
Weigeat, Johann Blasius 96
Whalingman 47
Wheatstone, Charles 93
Windsor 11
Winkler, Frans 14
Wischer, J. 102
Wood, Small & Co. 76
Wurlitzer 51

Zanoli, G.B. 113, 119
Zind Gion 89
Zithers 122
Zonophone 32
Zuleger & Mayenburg 93
Zumpe, Johannes 83